Praise for *Talking to Siri®, Second Edition*

"So you think you know everything that Siri can do? I'll bet you don't. What you can accomplish with Siri is amazing if you just know how to ask, and this book is where you will learn what to say and how to say it. With generous illustrations and simple explanations, Erica and Steve will help you get more out of Siri. Much more."

—Chuck Joiner, MacVoices

"It's easy to dismiss Siri as a fun novelty that gives amusing answers to 'Open the pod bay doors, Siri.' But Siri is a remarkably useful tool. The authors of *Talking to Siri* make it fast and easy to learn how to put it to use, whether that's the quickest way to call your husband, schedule a reminder ('When I get home, remind me to...'), or find out the baseball score. The writing is delightful, and the information full of 'Gosh, how cool!'"

—Esther Schindler, Technology Journalist

"Steve and Erica's knowledge of Siri is surpassed only by the clarity with which they explain it. I learned several new tricks, even as a long-time Siri user."

—Dave Caolo, News Editor, *The Unofficial Apple Weblog*

Talking to **Siri**®

Learning the Language of
Apple®'s Intelligent Assistant
Second Edition

Erica Sadun
Steve Sande

que®
800 East 96th Street,
Indianapolis, Indiana 46240 USA

Talking to Siri®
Learning the Language of Apple®'s Intelligent Assistant

Copyright © 2013 by Erica Sadun and Steve Sande

All rights reserved. No part of this book shall be reproduced, stored in a retrieval system, or transmitted by any means, electronic, mechanical, photocopying, recording, or otherwise, without written permission from the publisher. No patent liability is assumed with respect to the use of the information contained herein. Although every precaution has been taken in the preparation of this book, the publisher and author assume no responsibility for errors or omissions. Nor is any liability assumed for damages resulting from the use of the information contained herein.

ISBN-13: 978-0-7897-5069-3
ISBN-10: 0-7897-5069-4

The Library of Congress cataloging-in-publication data is on file.

Printed in the United States of America

First Printing: January 2013

Trademarks

All terms mentioned in this book that are known to be trademarks or service marks have been appropriately capitalized. Que Publishing cannot attest to the accuracy of this information. Use of a term in this book should not be regarded as affecting the validity of any trademark or service mark.

Siri is a trademark of Apple, Inc.

Day-Timer is a registered trademark of ACCO Brands Corporation.

Warning and Disclaimer

Every effort has been made to make this book as complete and as accurate as possible, but no warranty or fitness is implied. The information provided is on an "as is" basis. The authors and the publisher shall have neither liability nor responsibility to any person or entity with respect to any loss or damages arising from the information contained in this book or from the use of programs accompanying it.

Talking to Siri is an independent publication and has not been authorized, sponsored, or otherwise approved by Apple, Inc.

Bulk Sales

Que Publishing offers excellent discounts on this book when ordered in quantity for bulk purchases or special sales. For more information, please contact

U.S. Corporate and Government Sales
1-800-382-3419
corpsales@pearsontechgroup.com

For sales outside the United States, please contact

International Sales
international@pearson.com

Editor-in-Chief
Mark Taub

Senior Acquisitions Editor
Trina MacDonald

Senior Development Editor
Chris Zahn

Managing Editor
Kristy Hart

Project Editor
Jovana Shirley

Copy Editor
Krista Hansing Editorial Services, Inc.

Indexer
Erika Millen

Proofreader
Kathy Ruiz

Publishing Coordinator
Olivia Basegio

Book Designer
Anne Jones

Compositor
Nonie Ratcliff

Contents at a Glance

Preface xi

1 Getting Started with Siri 1

2 Asking Siri for Information 35

3 Using Siri to Stay in Touch 59

4 Talking to Your Day-Timer 81

5 Going Shopping with Siri 101

6 Pushing Limits with Siri 123

7 Siri Dictation 137

8 Having Fun with Siri 165

A Siri Quick Reference 187

Index 197

Table of Contents

Preface...xi

1 Getting Started with Siri..1

Enabling Siri on iOS..2
    Universal Access...6

Enabling Dictation on OS X...7

Privacy...9

Launching Siri on iOS..10
    Saying Hello to Siri..11
    Canceling Siri...13
    Repeating Siri...14
    Quitting Siri..14
    Getting Help...15

Siri Listens..17
    Listening on OS X...19
    Siri Responds..20

Correcting Siri...21
    Correcting Speech on OS X......................................23
    Enhancing Your Speech Recognition.......................24
    Clarity..25
    Fumbles..26
    Viewing Items You Create.......................................27
    Multilingual Siri...28

New in Siri..29
    Living with Siri Limitations....................................30
    Let Siri Learn About You...31

Summary..31

2 Asking Siri for Information..35

Weather...36
    Other Queries..37
    Locations...37

Web Search 39

    Searching for Pictures 41

    Searching in Wikipedia 41

    The Search the Web Option 42

    Checking Flights 42

Sports and Siri 43

Checking Stocks 46

Using Wolfram Alpha 48

    Querying Wolfram 50

    Wolfram Mode 52

    The Wolfram Saving Throw 52

    Wolfram Alpha Trick Lets You Know What Is

        Flying Overhead 53

    Other Cool Stuff You Can Do with Wolfram Alpha 55

Summary 56

3 Using Siri to Stay in Touch **59**

Contacts 60

    Searching for Contacts 62

    Creating Relationships 63

    Creating an Alternative Identity for Yourself 65

Placing Phone Calls with Siri 67

Text Messages 68

    Reading Texts 69

    Replying to Texts 70

    Sending Messages 70

    Confirming Messages 71

Mail 72

    Creating Mail 72

    Checking Mail 75

    Responding to Mail 75

Social Networking 75

Friends 76

Summary 79

4 Talking to Your Day-Timer **81**

Calendars 82
   Adding Events 82
   Making Changes 83
   Checking Your Calendar 84

Reminders 86
   How Siri Can Remind You 88
   A Word of Caution 89

Creating Notes 90
   Creating Single-Item Notes 90
   Adding Items to the Current Note 91
   Starting New Notes 92
   Naming Notes 92
   Finding Notes 93

Clock Functions 94
   Alarms 94
   Checking the Clock 97
   Using a Timer 97

Summary 99

5 Going Shopping with Siri **101**

Products and Services 102
   Checking Prices 104

Shopping Math 105
   Adding Sales Tax 105
   Calculating Tips 106
   Currency Conversion 107

Preparing a Shopping List 109

Sharing Shopping Lists via the Cloud 111
   Shopping Limitations 112

Turn-by-Turn Directions..113

    Using Turn-by-Turn to Known Destinations..................115

    Maps' Search and Directions Limitations......................115

    Looking up Information on Maps.......................................117

Making Restaurant Reservations...117

Checking out Movies..118

    Siri's Personal Movie Synopses.......................................120

Summary..121

6 Pushing Limits with Siri..**123**

Launching Apps..124

Talking to Apps...125

Blogging with Siri...126

    Creating a Post...126

    Confirming Your Account...128

    Blogging by Email..128

    Other Blogging Services...131

Siri Security...132

    Lock Screen and Siri..133

Music...134

Summary..136

7 Siri Dictation...**137**

Launching Dictation on iOS...138

Launching Dictation on OS X...138

Why Learn Dictation?...141

Enunciation Practice..142

Dictation 101...144

    Improving Dictation..144

Inserting Punctuation..147

    Controlling Flow...149

    Adding Capitalization...150

Including Abbreviations 152

Dictating Technical Terms 154
     Phone Numbers 155
     Dates and Times 155
     Prices 156

Smilies 157

Dictating Formatted Text 157
     Addresses 157
     URLs 158
     Email Addresses 158
     License Plates 159

Dictation Practice 159

Punctuation Practice 161

Summary 163

8   **Having Fun with Siri** **165**

Siri Diversions 165

Asking About Siri 167

Siri Chitchat 171

Pop Culture Fun 174

Siri Miscellany 175
     Siri Philosophy 178
     Mining the Fun in Wolfram Alpha 179
     Queries That Require Wolfram Prefixes 182

Summary 184

Appendix **187**

Siri Quick Reference 187

Index **197**

Preface

With Siri, your spoken wishes are your iPhone's command. Available on the newest iPhones (4S and later), iPads (third generation and later), iPad minis, and iPod Touches (fifth generation and later), the voice-operated Siri assistant uses natural-language processing to answer your questions, respond to your commands, and provide assistance as you need it. With Siri, you can set up meetings, call your mom, ask about your appointments, check your email, find your friends, and do a lot more.

Using Siri is incredibly convenient. You'll find yourself using your device in ways you never did before because Siri makes things so much simpler. "Wake me up at 8:30 a.m." "Tell my spouse I'm on my way home." "Remind me to stop by the dry cleaners when I leave here." "Text my hairdresser." Siri offers virtual concierge services that simplify your life.

This short book introduces you to Siri. You learn how to access the voice assistant by using the Home button and how to achieve the highest recognition rate as you talk. You discover which categories Siri responds to and find out how to make the most of each of these in your conversations. You also discover practical how-to guidance mixed with many examples to inspire as well as to instruct.

Tutorials show you how to set up Siri in your preferences and how to manage the interactive conversations you have with your voice assistant. You learn how to perform tasks by topic: checking the weather, doing math, or looking up information on the Web.

Siri dictation has now made the leap to OS X. Your Mac can listen to what you say and transcribe it in words to nearly any text-ready application. You can dictate letters, create notes, or specify reminder details with your voice. This book shows you how to control dictation—on both OS X and iOS—so you can add punctuation, paragraph breaks, and more.

Ready to get started? Here are all the basics you need for talking to Siri, presented in a simple, easy-to follow handbook.

What's New in This Edition

At Apple's WWDC 2012 Keynote, CEO Tim Cook introduced a refreshed generation of Siri. With new and expanded features, Siri now offers more consumer-centric capabilities for everyday use. From sports scores to restaurant reviews, movie listings to Facebook support, Siri has been updated to get more things done in more places around the world. Siri can now even launch applications!

This revised edition brings you all the helpful common-sense how-to that made the first edition of *Talking to Siri* a best seller. In addition, it introduces many new features to help both original users and those who just are getting to know Siri, especially as it extends to new devices such as the iPad.

But that's not all. Siri's dictation features are now available on Mac OS X Mountain Lion. This revised edition teaches dictation how-to across Apple's entire product line, not just for iPhones.

When you pick up this book, you'll be sure to learn some new tricks and discover what Siri can do to enhance your life.

Who This Book Is For

This book is written for anyone who has purchased a Siri-enabled iOS device or who owns a Mac running OS X Mountain Lion and wonders how to make the most of it. If you're looking for tips, tricks, and how-to guidance, you've come to the right place. This book offers friendly, easy-to-read tutorials that show you, with a wealth of examples, the ins and outs of Siri use in real life.

How This Book Is Organized

This book offers topic-by-topic coverage of basic Siri usage. Each chapter groups related tasks together, allowing you to jump directly to the material you're looking for. Here's a rundown of what you find in this book's chapters.

- **Chapter 1, "Getting Started with Siri":** This chapter introduces you to Siri basics. You read about setting up the service, launching it, and trying it out. You discover how to speak clearly and how to recover from mistakes when Siri misunderstands you.

- **Chapter 2, "Asking Siri for Information":** Want to check the weather or stocks? Need to search the Web? Eager to find out whether your favorite team is winning? This chapter introduces ways you can check information by conversing with Siri. You read about Siri integration with Wikipedia and Wolfram Alpha and learn how to ask questions that get you the best possible answers.

- **Chapter 3, "Using Siri to Stay in Touch":** This chapter shows you how you can use Siri queries to keep in touch with your friends, family, and business contacts. You read about searching for contacts, placing phone calls, texting, tweeting, updating Facebook, and sending email. You learn about how Siri relationships work and how you can let Siri know who your spouse, your child, or your parent is.

- **Chapter 4, "Talking to Your Day-Timer":** When you want to create appointments, take notes, or set reminders, Siri provides the perfect set of tools for organizing your life. Siri enables you to check your daily schedule, jot down important notes, and set short-term timers and alarms. This chapter introduces all the ways you can use Siri to help schedule and organize your life.

- **Chapter 5, "Going Shopping with Siri":** Whether you're searching for goods and services, trying to find your way to local businesses, or trying to figure out tax and tip after eating lunch, Siri has the tools you need. In this chapter, you read about using Siri to go shopping. You discover great ways to hunt down the items you need (including turn-by-turn directions!) and surprisingly useful tips on having Siri remind you about them when you get close to the stores that carry them.

- **Chapter 6, "Pushing Limits with Siri":** The Siri universe continues to expand over time. With a little clever work, you can blog using Siri text messaging and email. This chapter shows you how you can push the Siri envelope.

- **Chapter 7, "Siri Dictation":** Siri does a lot more than just answer queries. Its built-in dictation support means you can use its natural language-to-text support to speak to applications on iOS or Mac OS X. This chapter discusses all the ins and outs of Siri dictation, providing tips and hints about getting the most accurate responses, and shows how you can produce exactly the text you're looking to create (punctuation and all).

- **Chapter 8, "Having Fun with Siri":** In this chapter, you read about having fun with Siri and all the clever ways you can tickle your personal assistant's funny bone. It's okay to be silly with Siri. This chapter shows you how.

- **Appendix: "Siri Quick Reference":** This appendix provides a topic-by-topic list of things you can say to Siri, offering you an overview of this highly capable assistant's capabilities.

Contacting the Authors

If you have any comments or questions about this book, please visit http://sanddunetech.com/contact-us/. We're happy to listen to your feedback. Follow us on Twitter (@sanddunebooks) to keep up with our new ebooks.

About the Authors

Erica Sadun writes a lot of books and blogs at TUAW. When not writing, she's a full-time parent of geeks who are brushing up on their world-domination skills. According to her academic dosimeter, she's acquired more education than any self-respecting person might consider wise. She enjoys deep-diving into technology.

Steve Sande also writes way too much. He's the hardware editor at TUAW and has logged more than 1.5 million words written for the blog in a little more than 4 years. He's written a number of books for Take Control Books and Apress, is married to a rocket scientist, and spends his days being bossed by a cat.

Acknowledgments

We want to thank Megan Lavey-Heaton for her help on the cover for this book and to Mike Rose for his help with edits. Thanks, too, to everyone at TUAW for all their support and to all the readers and friends who helped with suggestions and feedback. Additional thanks for this edition go out to Aaron Kulbe and Matt Yohe.

None of this would have been possible without the vision and leadership of Apple's late founder and CEO, Steve Jobs. Thank you, Mr. Jobs.

We Want to Hear from You!

As the reader of this book, *you* are our most important critic and commentator. We value your opinion and want to know what we're doing right, what we could do better, what areas you'd like to see us publish in, and any other words of wisdom you're willing to pass our way.

We welcome your comments. You can email or write to let us know what you did or didn't like about this book—as well as what we can do to make our books better.

Please note that we cannot help you with technical problems related to the topic of this book.

When you write, please be sure to include this book's title and author, as well as your name, email address, and phone number. I will carefully review your comments and share them with the author and editors who worked on the book.

Email: errata@informit.com

Mail: Que Publishing
ATTN: Reader Feedback
1330 Avenue of the Americas
35th Floor
New York, New York, 10019

Reader Services

Visit our website and register this book at informit.com/register for convenient access to any updates, downloads, or errata that might be available for this book.

Getting Started with Siri

Have you met Siri? If you own a current-generation iOS device, this virtual assistant is waiting for your command. Siri runs on the iPhone (4S or later), iPod touch (fifth generation or later), and iPad (third generation or later).

On iOS, Siri replaces the dance of your fingers on the glass screen of the device with a conversation like the one in Figure 1-1. Siri understands your voice, places what you say in context to the apps that it works with, and even responds with a question if it doesn't understand. For the first time outside science fiction, we have a way to interface in natural language with a computer.

Siri doesn't stop there. If you own an OS X Mountain Lion Macintosh computer, you have access to Siri dictation as well. You can speak to dictate emails, create reports with your voice, and more.

Figure 1-1
Siri awaits your command.

In this chapter, you learn how to get started with Siri: how to enable it, launch the service, and try it out. You read about how to speak (slowly and clearly), how to recover from mistakes (Siri lets you edit errors), and how to access the service in a variety of ways. By the time you finish reading this chapter, you'll feel at ease talking to (instead of at) Siri.

Enabling Siri on iOS

To ensure that the Siri service has been enabled, navigate to Settings, General, Siri. Here you find a screen of options, as shown in Figure 1-2. These options let you control how Siri works. Use this screen to adjust the way Siri is set up and responds to you.

Figure 1-2
From the Siri Preferences pane, you can choose a primary language, set when you want the service to speak to you, and enable or disable the Raise to Speak option. Some options vary by iOS device. Only the iPhone supports Raise to Speak. Other devices do not offer proximity sensors.

Switch the primary Siri toggle to On to activate the service. On the iPhone, when the service is disabled, the older iOS VoiceControl feature still enables you to place hands-free calls and request music. Siri is much more powerful than VoiceControl and offers a wider range of voice-directed actions.

Disabling Siri is not a step you take lightly. Doing so removes your information from Apple servers. If you want to reenable Siri later, reestablishing your personal profile might take time (see Figure 1-3).

The other options you find on this settings page include the following:

- **Language:** Select the language and region you want Siri to use for interpreting your interaction. In its initial release, Siri supported only English (U.S., U.K., and Australia), French, and German. The set of supported languages and regions grew over time as Siri was deployed throughout the world. Siri now speaks Japanese, Spanish, Italian, Korean, Mandarin, and Cantonese, with Apple rolling out more languages and dialects over time. You can ask Siri, "What languages do you speak?" and see them listed.

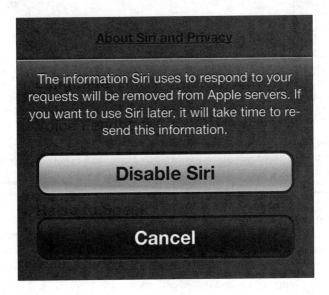

Figure 1-3
When you disable Siri, you delete information stored on Apple's servers. Siri has to relearn your personal style if you reenable it in the future.

- **Voice Feedback:** Decide whether you want Siri to respond to you with voice as well as text responses. You can choose to always enable this feature (Always) or to support it only for hands-free operation (Handsfree Only) when used with a headset of some sort.

  If you choose Always, remember that Siri uses a volume control system that's separate from your main iOS device (see Figure 1-4). Lowering the loudness of your music playback won't affect Siri, and vice versa. If you enable voice feedback and forget to lower the Siri volume, you could encounter embarrassing situations. Imagine being in a meeting and activating the service by accident. You set Siri's volume by opening the assistant (press and hold the Home button or raise the unit to your ear) and then adjusting the device's volume toggles.

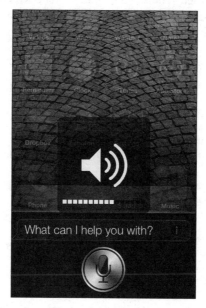

Figure 1-4
Siri has its own volume controls. Adjusting the volume when Siri is displayed does not affect normal iOS system volume, and vice versa.

- **My Info:** This sets the default contact for your identity from your personal address book. Choosing a contact lets Siri knows where "home" is, what your name is, and so forth. It also allows Siri to associate relationships with your contacts, such as "my spouse" or "my boss" or "my doctor." Make sure this option points to the right contact so that when Siri tries to help you, it's working with the right person.

- **Raise to Speak:** (*iPhone only*) When enabled, Siri activates using the iPhone proximity sensor. This feature is not available on iPod touch and iPad units. This is the onboard sensor that detects when your face is near the iPhone screen. By switching this setting to On, you can start a Siri session by raising the iPhone to your ear. You generally want to leave this option enabled. It offers the simplest and most discrete way to activate Siri from your handset.

 NOTE

Muting your iOS device and lowering the speaker volume to zero does not directly affect Siri chimes for either dictation or voice assistance. If you hold the Home key for too long or your finger brushes across the microphone in the keyboard, you could trigger a Siri-based beep. This can be quite embarrassing in boardroom or classroom situations. That's because Siri has its own volume control (see Figure 1-4), which you access only when the assistant is shown onscreen.

To adjust Siri's volumes settings, summon your personal assistant and then adjust the volume control when the purple microphone is onscreen. You can silence Siri here, ensuring that your Siri-enabled device stays quiet even when you accidentally open the assistant screen. This doesn't affect the chime Siri plays (just to you) when you hold a phone to your ear.

Universal Access

Siri works with VoiceOver, the screen reader built into iOS. VoiceOver offers a way for visually impaired users to "listen" to their *graphical user interface* (GUI). VoiceOver converts an application's visual presentation to an audio description.

VoiceOver can speak any text displayed on your iOS screen, including Siri responses. VoiceOver speech can also interpret as speech certain graphical elements presented by Siri. These include weather forecasts, email bodies, answers from Wolfram Alpha, and so forth.

You enable VoiceOver in Settings, General, Accessibility, VoiceOver. Be sure to set the Triple-Click Home option to On so that you can enable and disable VoiceOver with a simple shortcut.

When using VoiceOver, you use the iPhone GUI with your fingers and ears rather than with your eyes. An entire language of touches is used with VoiceOver, with a challenging learning curve. Consult documentation on Apple's website for details about using VoiceOver features both in general and with Siri.

Enabling Dictation on OS X

Starting with OS X Mountain Lion, you can use Siri-style dictation on your Macintosh. You enable this feature in the System Preferences Dictation & Speech pane (see Figure 1-5). Setting the Dictation option to On activates dictation services on your computer. These services enable you to speak text wherever you would normally type it.

The Shortcut pop-up menu lets you choose how to begin dictation. In Figure 1-5, this shortcut is set to Press Right Command Key Twice. Other preset options enable you to press the function (Fn) key twice, the left command key twice, or (our favorite) either command key twice.

If you'd rather use a nonstandard key choice, choose Customize from the pop-up menu and type a different key or key combination. For example, you might use Shift-F6 or Control-Shift-D. You choose the key combination that best fits your personal workflow.

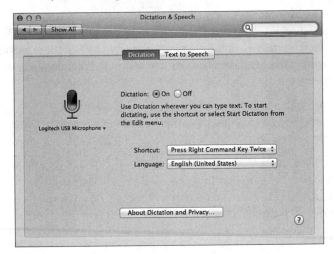

Figure 1-5
OS X's Dictation & Speech settings pane enables you to activate dictation on your Macintosh.

Select the dictation language and region from the Language pop-up menu. OS X Mountain Lion currently supports English, French, German, and Japanese. This set will almost certainly grow over time.

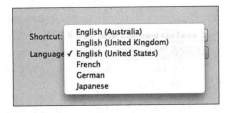

Figure 1-6
OS X dictation currently offers a limited number of languages and regions.

NOTE

Many Siri services are country and region specific. Some
features, such as dictation, are available practically worldwide.
Others, such as maps and directions, have been rolled out on a
far more limited basis. Check Apple's website to see if specific
Siri features are available in your area.

Privacy

Apple collects data on your Siri usage. Information sent to Apple
includes your contacts in the address book, your name and
contact information, songs and playlists from your media library,
audio recordings of you speaking, transcripts of what you have
said, and operating system information/performance statistics. If
you use Siri, a lot of your personal information goes to Apple.

What's more, this information may be shared with Apple's
partners for dictation-related services, but it is not shared with
other third parties. You cannot opt out of data collection, but you
can opt out of Siri entirely by not using the feature and disabling
it in Settings or System Preferences.

If you don't mind having Apple collect information on you, but
you want to opt out your children, you can separately control
access to Dictation in the Parental Controls pane.

For more about Siri privacy issues, tap the About Siri and Privacy
link in the iOS Siri Settings pane or the About Dictation and
Privacy link in the OS X Dictation & Speech pane. Figure 1-7 shows
the privacy disclosure screens for iOS and OS X.

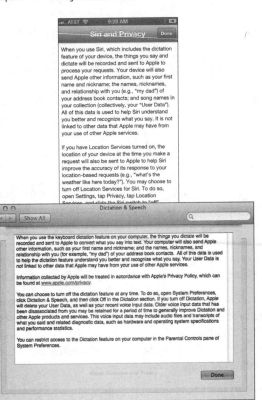

Figure 1-7
Apple collects a lot of information when you use Siri.

Launching Siri on iOS

On iOS, Siri lets you use your voice instead of your fingers to send messages, schedule meetings, choose music, and more. You use Siri conversationally. You talk to your device, and your device talks right back to you.

You can access Siri in several ways:

- Press and hold the Home button for a couple seconds.
- Raise your iPhone to your ear. *(Not available on iPod touch or iPad.)*
- Engage it from your wired (iPhone earbud style) or wireless (Bluetooth) headset by squeezing or pressing the control button. Siri also works with many car kits. A small blue speaker icon appears in Siri's display when you connect through Bluetooth.

A chime tells you that Siri is listening and ready to follow your commands. Make sure that Siri is enabled and that you've got a good Internet connection. If so, you are ready to take off and start exploring this innovative voice-driven service.

 NOTE

An independent start-up founded by the Stanford Research Institute's Artificial Intelligence Center created Siri's recognition technology in 2007 (hence the name Siri). Apple acquired the Siri company in 2010 and first debuted the technology in iOS 5 on the iPhone 4S.

 NOTE

This book refers to Siri as *it*, not as *him* or *her*. This is because Siri has many voices, which are tied to localizations. These voices vary in gender based on the region in use. For example, in the United States, the default Siri voice is female; in the United Kingdom, it is male.

Saying Hello to Siri

Siri uses several chimes. These audio cues let you know when Siri is listening to you. A higher chime starts a session, and a lower one cancels it. To hear this on the iPhone if you have Raise to Speak enabled, raise your phone (turned on, of course) to your ear and then place it back on a table. The high chirps mean Siri is listening; the low chirps mean it has stopped listening. On the iPod touch or iPad, press and hold the Home button (high chirp) and then tap the Siri microphone (low chirp).

Try the following: First, start a Siri session. Either raise the phone to your ear or press and hold the Home button. If Siri is already displayed, tap the Siri microphone button.

Say "Hello," and then pause. Siri uses pause detection to know when you've stopped speaking. You now hear a second set of chirps—a higher-pitched chirp of acknowledgment, in this case—but this time you hear them without moving the phone away from your ear or having to tap the microphone button.

If you have a good Internet connection—a requirement of working with Siri—you'll hear it respond to you. Siri responds with "Hi" or "Hello," perhaps adding your name (see Figure 1-8). As you talk, Siri creates a scrolling list of responses so you can review the conversation to date. By default, Siri automatically scrolls up to the most recent response, so you might want to pull down on the list to see what has transpired before.

To summarize, you can start talking to Siri in these ways:

- Pressing and holding the Home button for 1 to 2 seconds
- Raising a phone to your ear
- Tapping the Siri microphone button

Siri plays chimes that indicate the state of your interaction. By listening for these chimes, you'll know how Siri is responding to you.

- Its higher-pitched "listening" chime (a C#4 for the musically inclined) lets you know Siri's ready for you to speak.

- To finish talking, you can either pause or tap the microphone button. Siri plays a high-pitched "done listening" chime (a higher A♭4).

- If Siri does not hear any input, it stops listening and plays a lower-pitched "cancellation" chime (a lower A♭3).

Figure 1-8
Saying hello to Siri.

Canceling Siri

If you ever need to stop whatever Siri is doing, just say "Cancel" and then either tap the microphone button or press the Home button.

Because Siri remembers your ongoing thread of conversation, you might need to reset your current conversation at times. Say "Start over" or "Restart" to begin a new dialogue. Siri responds with a response such as, "Okay, Erica, what's next?" or "What can I help you with?"

Repeating Siri

When you did not quite catch what Siri last said, say "Say it again." Siri repeats its last response. This feature gives you a second chance for comprehension, or offers you the possibility to repeat a particularly clever punch line to share with others.

Quitting Siri

Leave Siri mode by pressing the Home button or saying "Goodbye." This returns you to your normal iOS home screen. If you say "Quit," Siri responds, "Did I say something wrong? If you really want me to go away, at least say 'Goodbye.'" and "Quit? Did you mean 'Goodbye'?" (See Figure 1-9.)

Asking Siri to "go away" or "leave" won't work, but you can say any of the following to exit Siri mode.

- Goodbye
- Bye
- Bye-bye
- So long
- Adios
- See you later
- See you

Figure 1-9
To leave Siri mode by voice, say "Goodbye." Asking Siri to quit or go away does not end your Siri interaction.

Getting Help

Siri provides suggestions on what to say. Just say "Help me" or "What can you do?" Siri displays a list of categories, such as Phone, Music, Messages, and Calendar, along with a sample phrase for each topic, which you see in Figure 1-10. Tap on any category to view an extended list of sample phrases for just that category.

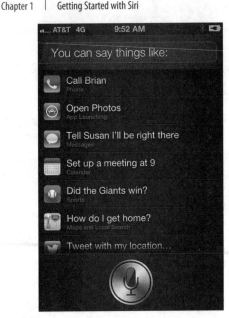

Figure 1-10

Not sure what to say to Siri? Siri can offer suggestions. Just say "Help" or "What can you do?" A tiny *i* appears at the right of Siri's first "What can I help you with" message whenever you invoke it. You can see this in Figure 1-11. You can also tap this i to request this help screen.

For example, if you're interested in contacts, you tap What's Emily's Address. Siri then offers the following examples. They provide a range of functions that showcase how you can interactively ask about the people in your address book.

- What's Emily's address?
- What is Susan Park's phone number?
- When is my wife's birthday?
- Show Lindsey's home email address.
- What's my brother's work address?

- Show Brian Conway.
- Find people named Park.
- Who is Jimmy Patrick?
- My mom is Susan Park.
- Jimmy Patrick is my brother.
- Call my brother at work.

This onboard help system lets you know the kinds of interactions that Siri supports. They inspire you to expand your Siri vocabulary and use the assistant system more flexibly.

Siri Listens

As Siri listens to you speaking, look at the microphone in the center of the Siri button at the bottom of the screen (see Figure 1-11, top). This microphone acts as a level meter for your spoken input. It provides you with volume feedback as you speak and lets you know that Siri is in listening mode. If you do not respond after a few seconds, Siri stops listening and plays the end-of-listening chime.

To finish speaking, either pause and wait for Siri or tap the Siri button. After listening, Siri enters thinking mode. During this time, a purple glow circles the button, letting you know that Siri is contacting Apple's data centers for speech interpretation and processing (see Figure 1-11, bottom).

Siri works with both 3G and Wi-Fi Internet connections, so you can use it wherever you are. The data demands are fairly minimal, so you probably do not need to worry about depleting your monthly allocation by using Siri too much.

Figure 1-11
Top: Siri's microphone button acts as a level meter. The purple bar rises and falls with your speech.
Bottom: A purple light circles the microphone button as Siri contacts its servers to interpret your speech.

If Siri is able to process your statement, it tries to interpret it and provide some kind of response for you. If Siri cannot call home to its Apple data processing center, it informs you about the situation, saying something like, "I'm sorry, I'm having difficulty accessing the network." Try moving to a location with a better Internet signal or try again later.

 NOTE

On iOS, Siri works with many audio accessories, including Apple's iPhone earbuds (the ones with the built-in microphone and squeeze control), Bluetooth headsets, and car stereo kits.

At Apple's 2012 Worldwide Developer's Conference, Apple announced that it was working with a number of automobile manufacturers to add an "Eyes Free" button to car steering wheels for enabling Siri safely while driving.

Listening on OS X

On OS X, the Siri microphone works much the same as it does under iOS. As Figure 1-12 shows, the microphone acts as a level meter, and an animated dot presentation shows that the computer is actively contacting servers for speech interpretation. OS X does not use pause detection, so you must either click Done or press Return to finish your dictation.

Figure 1-12
Top: The microphone on OS X also works as a level meter. The purple bar's height reflects the current volume of your speech. Bottom: OS X's trio of dots lets you know that Siri is contacting servers to interpret your speech. The purple dot cycles from left to right during this time.

Siri Responds

Siri responds to both direct commands and random statements. If what you said cannot be interpreted as a request, Siri offers to search the Web for your statement. For example, Figure 1-13 shows how Siri responds to the word *platypuses*. If you choose Search the Web, Siri uses your word or phrase for a web search using your default engine. Set your default search engine in Settings, Safari, Search Engine, and choose from Google, Yahoo!, or Bing.

Figure 1-13
Siri offers web searches for any words or phrases it doesn't immediately recognize.

NOTE

Siri learns your accent and voice characteristics over time. As long as you keep Siri enabled in your iPhone settings, your Siri account remains on Apple's servers and your recognition rates improve over time. Siri uses voice-recognition algorithms to categorize your voice into its database of regional dialects and accents. This database continues to evolve and will keep improving as Siri collects more data and evaluates its interpretation successes. Siri also uses information from your iPhone. Data from your contacts, music library, calendar, and reminders helps fuel its recognition vocabulary.

To reset your Siri information, switch Siri off and then back on in Settings, General, Siri. This disposes of all personalized settings Siri has collected from you over time (not including any general metrics it studies and adds to its primary database) and returns Siri to a fresh install, ready to learn your quirks again.

Correcting Siri

Siri always gives you a second chance. To fix what you said or correct Siri's interpretation of your speech, just tap the speech bubble that represents what you said (see Figure 1-14). When you do, the bubble turns white and the system keyboard appears. At this point, you can type directly into the bubble. You can edit your request directly or tap the microphone button on the keyboard to redictate your request. Tap Done to finish.

Sometimes Siri's dictation processor adds a blue line under a word in the text you have spoken. When you tap that word, iOS presents alternative interpretations of your speech. Select the correction you want to use or edit, or dictate a replacement.

You can also speak to correct text messages or mail contents that you have composed. The following statements let Siri know that you're not satisfied with what you've said. Notice how you can change the contents completely, add new material, and more:

- Change it to: Let's meet at 3:00 p.m.
- Add: Can't wait exclamation point. (You can use Add to extend items, even if Siri doesn't mention it explicitly as an option.)
- No, send it to Megs.
- No. (This keeps the message without sending it.)
- Cancel.

Figure 1-14
Tap your speech bubble to edit it directly or redictate your statement.

Before you send a text message on its way, have Siri read it back to you. Say "Read it to me" or "Read it back to me." As with the

Add feature, Siri does not tell you about this option. When you are satisfied with your text or email message, say something like "Yes, send it" to send it off.

Correcting Speech on OS X

The same dashed underlines appear on OS X as you see in iOS. Because OS X is centered on the mouse, not the touch, the methods for accessing variant spellings differ. Figure 1-15 shows the result of saying "I'm ready to dictate now." Siri has misinterpreted the last word but flagged it with possible variations. It shows this flag by underlining the word with a dashed blue line.

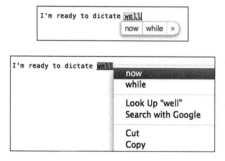

Figure 1-15
Under OS X, you can either left-click just to the right of an underlined word (top) or right-click the underlined word (bottom).

If you move the cursor to the very right of the word in question and left-click, OS X presents a list of alternative interpretations. That's *now* and *while* for this example. Tap either word to choose. OS X replaces the word with your selection and removes the underline.

You can also right-click (Control-click) the underlined word to bring up a contextual menu. The alternate interpretations are listed at the top of the menu. Select one to confirm and replace.

Alternatively, you can simply type to correct the text. Dictating and then correcting by hand offers a robust workflow for both OS X and iOS.

Enhancing Your Speech Recognition

On iOS, Siri responds to commands by creating appointments, setting timers, placing phone calls, and more. To see this in action, try creating a new note on your iOS device. Say, "Note that I spent $15 on lunch." Speak steadily, but do not draaaaag oooooooout what you're saying. Siri should reply, "Noted" or "Got it!" or something like that (see Figure 1-16). On OS X, you use the same approach: Use steady, clear sentences.

When talking to Siri, remain conversational. Try to speak with normal tones and inflections, although you'll want to slow down slightly. Enunciate a bit more than you're used to, like a pedantic teacher. The key to Siri is holding on to your standard speech patterns while emphasizing any words that help Siri understand you better.

Don't be afraid to ask questions (with your voice rising at the end), make statements (with your voice dropping), or otherwise speak sentences as you normally do, including emphasizing words inside sentences (for example, "What does *intransigent* mean?"). Do not try to be robotic or lose normal sentence inflections. Your recognition rate will plummet if you do.

Figure 1-16
Siri can take notes to help you keep track of your expenses.

On iOS, this particular query should load up a definition, as shown in Figure 1-17. It's actually a little hard to speak this request coherently and in a way that Siri understands, so it makes a good exercise to test out your speaking skills.

Clarity

Siri likes to hear you speak slowly and clearly and prefers to have you e-nun-ci-ate your words, especially with word-ending consonants. This helps Siri differentiate between, for example, *me* and *mean*. This is an important distinction when defining words, as in this example with *intransigent*, because asking Siri "What does *intransigent* me?" won't load the dictionary definition you're looking for—but asking "What does *intransigent* mean?" does.

Figure 1-17
Use slow, careful speech to increase Siri's recognition rate, as in this word definition request.

Don't be afraid to add a little extra pause between words so that Siri can tell the difference between "Mike Rose" and "micros," or "Mike Rose's phone" and "microphone."

If you add too long of a pause, Siri stops listening, but that does not happen accidentally. A good deal of usable range exists between your normal speaking speed and the extreme at which Siri thinks you're not talking anymore. Explore that range and test longer pauses to see how you can improve your recognition.

Fumbles

Everybody fumbles words sometimes. If you find yourself stumbling over a tongue twister, either edit your current entry or cancel it entirely. On iOS, tap the microphone twice. The first tap ends your entry. The second cancels the current processing. The rotating purple "thinking" animation stops, and the microphone button returns to its quiescent state, letting you know that Siri is ready and waiting for your next command. On OS X, click Done and then Cancel.

Never worry about starting your request over. Siri doesn't care, and you can save a lot of time that would otherwise be wasted editing or waiting on interpretations of flubbed speech that are bound to go wrong.

Viewing Items You Create

Earlier, you read about how you might create a note using Siri. You can jump from Siri to the Notes application with a single tap. Just tap any yellow Siri note item. That is also where you need to go if you want to delete the note you just created. Siri does not enable you to delete notes directly, as you can see in Figure 1-18. That's because, as an assistant, Siri is directed toward creating new requests (notes, appointments, phone calls, dictation, weather checks) and not toward editing or application control in general. Siri is not a full voice interface.

The philosophy behind Siri is to offer a tool that enables you to accomplish simple creation and checking tasks hands free while on the go. But that's where Siri's capabilities end. Don't expect to navigate through menus, search for information within documents, or otherwise treat Siri as a full artificially intelligent user interface. Knowing what Siri can and cannot do helps limit your expectations while using this tool.

This tapping trick works with most Siri items, not just notes: Tap on contacts to view them in the Contacts app, or text messages in Messages, and so on. Siri often gives you items to choose from and actions to perform as well; tap on these choices to select a contact or perform web searches. You can also instruct Siri by voice, specifying how you want to proceed.

Figure 1-18
Siri can create notes but cannot delete them.

Multilingual Siri

Unfortunately, the Siri voice assistant cannot directly switch languages. The only way to change from English to French, for example, is to hop out, edit your preferences, and hop back in (Settings, General, International, Voice Control, Siri).

A workaround for multilanguage dictation exists, however. The Settings, General, International, Keyboards preferences allow you to add keyboards, enabling the globe button; when it is enabled, you can toggle directly between keyboard languages. You'll find it between the number toggle (123) and the microphone dictation button on the keyboard when you've enabled more than one language on your device.

A simple tap takes you to the next language setting, including dictation. By tapping, you move from French to English and back as you dictate into any text-entry element on your iPhone. Hopefully, Siri will support "Speak to me in [some language]" requests in a future update.

Siri recognizes each language using specific dialects and accents. Native speakers will experience higher recognition accuracy.

New in Siri

Siri is an evolving system. Apple continues to add new and exciting technologies to Siri, which it is rolling out over time. Figure 1-19 showcases the apps and services that Siri works with at the time this book was being written.

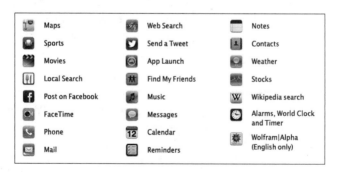

Figure 1-19
Siri integrates with a growing range of apps and services.

New standout features include sports: You can ask for the latest scores and statistics for your favorite teams and players. "How are the Bronco's doing?" or "Did the Mets win?"

Siri now provides movie reviews and showtimes, too. Say, "What's playing nearby?" or "Is *The Bourne Legacy* any good?" Siri will show the hours the movie is playing and offer links to Rotten Tomato reviews.

Feeling hungry? Siri now integrates with Open Table so that you can make restaurant reservations and look up local reviews for nearby options.

In addition, you can ask Siri to launch apps for you. Just say "Open Angry Birds" or "Launch Puzzle Craft."

Living with Siri Limitations

A year after its launch, Siri remains a beta product, flaws and all. Even when it is mature, you can still expect that the voice-interpretation system will be subject to mistakes. After all, humans misunderstand things all the time. With the best of intentions and the best of interpretations, Siri will never be able to provide 100 percent accuracy. Consider Figure 1-20, which shows perfectly how Siri might always be limited.

Erica wanted Siri to play *Pachelbel Canon in D*. Instead, Siri offered to search for local Taco Bells. The similarity in phonemes, the basic units of speech used to construct the two phrases *Pachelbel* and *Taco Bell*, meant that Siri's algorithms had to pick from two possible interpretations. It went with the latter as more likely, even though Erica intended the former.

Figure 1-20
Here you can see what Erica meant (top) and what Siri interpreted (bottom).

Let Siri Learn About You

The more you use Siri, the better it understands you. Siri learns your regional accent over time and characterizes your voice into a specific dialect. This helps it improve its interpretation over time. What's more, Siri uses information from your device, including contacts, your music, your calendar, and your reminders, to better match what you're saying to what you mean.

Summary

Siri provides a new and natural way to interact with a computer, enabling you to speak and be understood. On iOS, Siri listens to your commands and then performs your bidding, responding through speech or a visual answer on the device screen.

On OS X, Siri enables you to dictate into any application that normally offers text input. Some key points to take away from this chapter are as follows:

- Think carefully about the information you are sending to Apple when you agree to enable Siri. That's a lot of personal information you are trusting Apple with. Most people won't be bothered by this, but you should make an informed choice, nonetheless.

- If you don't know what to say, ask Siri, "Help me," or tap the small *i* that appears on the first speech bubble of each session. Siri is always happy to provide a list of categories and sample phrases.

- You access Siri by pressing and holding the Home button, raising your iPhone to your ear, or squeezing or pressing the control button on a wired or wireless headset. On OS X, you customize how to trigger dictation through the Dictation & Speech control pane.

- Talk slowly and clearly to Siri. Siri works best when you enunciate deliberately.

- Remember that Siri is more about creating items than editing them. Build new appointments, create new notes, and write emails, but don't expect to cancel, delete, undo, or modify those items using the Siri interface.

- Siri talk bubbles typically lead to more actions, enabling you to jump into associated apps such as the Notes app for notes or the Contacts apps for addresses. You can tap both on your own talk bubbles and the ones Siri speaks to you.

- Don't be afraid of making mistakes with Siri. You can always reset your conversation or edit your speech bubble. Siri is designed to assist you, not to put obstacles in your way. Siri lets you add new text, edit the text you've already spoken, or redo your dictation from scratch. Use these tools to achieve the highest possible recognition rate.

- Siri uses a separate audio volume system. So if you're at a movie or a conference, make sure you mute your system audio *and* lower Siri's volume control. To do that, invoke Siri and use the volume toggles on the side of the phone to lower the Siri sound level.

- Siri simplifies your life. Whether it's setting alarms ("Wake me at 7:15"), finding a friend ("Where is Barbara Sande?"), or updating your family ("Message my husband I'm on the way"), Siri is there to help you become more productive with less work. The more you learn about using Siri, the simpler these tasks become over time. For so many of these items, the issue isn't whether Siri can handle those tasks; it's whether you know that they're there to use them. If this book helps you add a few essential ideas into your day-to-day Siri use, then we've proudly done our jobs.

Asking Siri for Information

Siri exists to serve you. It wants nothing more than to give you information about just about anything in the universe. Siri provides you with answers to questions about everything from the weather to stock prices through integration with the apps that come with your iOS device.

Questions outside the realm of the built-in apps on iOS are no problem for Siri. It knows how to work with Wikipedia and Wolfram Alpha, and it searches the Web for the best possible answers to whatever you ask. In this chapter, you learn how to phrase your conversation with Siri to maximize the probability of getting an accurate and detailed answer.

Weather

Siri keeps on top of the weather forecast for you. When you ask, "Will it rain tonight?" (see Figure 2-1) or "What is the temperature?", Siri offers immediate feedback. Asking "What's the weather for this week?" provides the full weekly forecast.

As a rule, Siri replies with simple answers. If extensive charts are involved, you are prompted to look at the phone instead of just listening.

Figure 2-1
Siri can check the weather for you.

Other Queries

In addition to the current weather conditions, Siri provides sunrise and sunset times (for the current day only) and the phase of the moon (although Siri sometimes balks, depending on whether the information is available for the moon phase). You can even ask, "When will Jupiter (or Mars or Venus or the Moon or so on) rise?" to query about planets.

Siri has no access to past weather information and cannot check information such as sunrise/sunset times for the future. So you cannot ask, "When will the sun rise tomorrow?" If you do, Siri reports only today's time.

Locations

When you switch locations, make sure you let Siri know. When you ask about the high today in London and then ask about the local wind speed, Siri defaults to the London wind speed, not the local one, unless local for you *is* London. So go ahead and say, "What's the wind speed here?" rather than "What's the wind speed?" to make sure you correct for the previous query.

Siri always tries to retain context for your conversations, to make it easier for you to add brief questions without having to keep stating who, where, and when, but these assumptions work against you if you don't specify "here" or "now" when changing the topic.

The best questions to ask in hands-free mode are ones that evaluate the weather, using specific quantities (how cold is it, how warm is it, what is the wind chill) or that specify whether it will rain/be cold/be hot, and so on. Figure 2-2 shows this kind of question in action. Siri replies with a useful narrated response.

Figure 2-2
Siri can answer questions that evaluate the weather.

 NOTE

When temperatures drop fast, Siri may add a "Brr" to your
weather report.

Siri offers a wide vocabulary of weather-related conversation. You
can ask about forecasts using many approaches. Here are some
things you can say to Siri about the weather:

- What's the weather for today?/What's the weather for
  tomorrow?

- What's the weather in London?

- Should I take an umbrella tomorrow?

- Should I wear a coat tonight?/Can I wear a bikini?
- Is it raining in Paris?
- How hot is it today?/How cold is it?
- What is the wind speed?/What is the wind speed in London right now?
- What is the humidity?/What is the wind chill?
- Will it rain in Cupertino this week?
- Will there be a storm here?
- When will it snow here?
- Check next week's forecast for Burlington.
- What's the forecast for this evening?
- Will it snow this week in Denver?
- How's the weather in Tampa right now?
- How hot will it be in Palm Springs this weekend?
- What's the high for Anchorage on Thursday?
- What's the temperature outside?
- How windy is it out there?
- Is it nighttime in Paris?/When is sunrise in Paris?

Web Search

With Siri, you have the entire Web not just at your fingertips, but also at the tip of your tongue. With spoken phrases, you can ask Siri to search the Web and show you the information it finds.

Siri uses several key phrases to hunt for information on the Web. You can tell it, "Search the Web," "Search the Web for [topic]," or "I want to see websites about…," among other web-oriented queries. Here are examples of web search requests you might ask Siri to perform:

- Search the Web for Bora Bora.
- Search for vegetarian pasta recipes.
- Search the Web for best cable plans.
- Search for news about the World Cup.
- I want to see websites about ostriches.
- Show me websites about baseball.

What's more, any of iOS's three major search engines are usable when you make your queries, so Google, Yahoo!, and Bing are all valid sources for information. For example, you might "Yahoo! pickle recipes," "Google knitting," or "Bing Parry Grip" (see Figure 2-3).

Figure 2-3
You can use search engine names as request verbs with Siri.

Searching for Pictures

If you're looking specifically for pictures, there's a shortcut for that, too. Say, "I want to see pictures of [topic]." For example, you might request, "I want to see pictures of kittens" (see Figure 2-4).

Figure 2-4
Siri understands requests that start with "I want to see…" and conducts a meaningful web search for you.

Searching in Wikipedia

Siri offers full Wikipedia support in addition to direct search engine access. All you have to do is ask your question the right way. Here are some ways to ask for information from the vast treasure hoard of Wikipedia. Knowing that you have to specify

Wikipedia as part of your statement is the majority of the battle:

- Search Wikipedia for Abraham Lincoln.
- Look up snowballs in Wikipedia.
- Search for eagles in Wikipedia.

The Search the Web Option

Whenever Siri cannot immediately respond to your request, it offers a web search on the topic you requested. For example, if you say "donkey grommets," Siri says, "I don't know what that means."

It offers a Search the Web button, which you can tap, or you can say, "Search the web" (see Figure 2-5). This opens Safari and searches for the phrase you spoke, using your current default search engine.

Checking Flights

TUAW reader Harris Rydal sent us a terrific way to use Siri's built-in search features to check flights. This is an exceptional opportunity to take advantage of Siri-to-Safari tasking. Say, "Search the Web for flights from [city/airport] to [city/airport]." In Google, this brings up a list of flight times that day and the associated airline.

Unfortunately, you cannot use this for future flights at this time. You can say, "Search the Web for flights on December 18 from Denver to Charlotte," but you will just load a general web search for Denver/Charlotte flights.

Figure 2-5
Siri responds to unrecognized phrases by offering a web search. You can tap the Search the Web button or say "Search the Web" to begin a query using your default search engine.

Sports and Siri

If you're a sports fan, Siri brings scores, schedules, rosters, and more to your device. As Figure 2-6 shows, Siri has the goods on many major sports. You can ask about your favorite teams and their players and check when the next game will happen.

Figure 2-6
Siri knows how your favorite team did.

Siri primarily covers U.S. sports. As far as international coverage goes, Siri is limited to football, what the U.S. calls "soccer." So although Siri knows about English Premiere League football, it has no knowledge of rugby or cricket, as it will tell you if you ask about those sports. Siri currently provides information for the following sports leagues.

- **Baseball**: Major League Baseball
- **U.S. Football**: NCAA football, National Football League
- **Basketball**: NCAA basketball, National Basketball Association, Women's National Basketball Association
- **Hockey**: National Hockey League

- **International Football (Soccer):** Italian Seria A, English Premier League, Dutch Eredivisie, Major League Soccer, French Ligue 1, Spanish La Liga, and German Bundesliga

Of these sports, Siri can respond to questions about scores, standings, team rosters, player stats, and playing schedules. Here are some of the specific ways you can ask Siri about sports.

- Did the Giants win?
- What was the score of the last Giants game?
- How did Kansas City do?
- What was the score the last time the Tigers played the Red Sox?
- What are the National League standings?
- Show me the football scores from last night.
- When do the Giants play next?
- How is Manchester United doing? (See Figure 2-7.)
- When is the Boston Red Sox's first game of the season?
- Show me the schedule for baseball.
- Who has the highest slugging percentage?
- What's Buster Posey's batting average?
- Who is taller, Lebron or Kobe?
- Who has the most home runs on the Giants?
- Who has the most goals in soccer?
- Which quarterback has the most passing yards?
- Show me the roster for the Dodgers.
- Who is pitching for the Miami Marlins this season?
- When is the Rockies' first game of the season?
- Is anyone on the Red Sox injured?

Figure 2-7
Siri displays the standings for many sports leagues but cannot guarantee that your favorite team will make the playoffs.

Checking Stocks

For those of us who have money in the stock market either through personal choice or with a 401(K) plan that was foisted on us at work, it's occasionally interesting to see how bad our investments are doing by checking on stock prices. Because a stock ticker is part of the iOS notification center and a Stocks app has been part of the iPhone since 2007, it's not surprising that Apple chose to have Siri be your personal investment assistant (see Figure 2-8).

Figure 2-8
Siri supplies up-to-the-minute information about the markets and individual stocks, but it won't tell you what to buy or sell.

Not only does Siri give you an overall snapshot of the market averages, but it also supplies details about individual stocks. Here's an overview of some of the phrases that Siri understands. Just ask about the company name, and Siri looks up the stock details.

- How is Proctor and Gamble doing?
- What's Coca-Cola trading at?
- What's Apple's stock price?
- What is Apple's PE ratio?
- What did Yahoo! close at today?

- How is the Nikkei doing?
- How are the markets doing?
- What is the Dow at?
- What did Apple close at?
- What was Apple's high this year?

If you say, "Buy 500 shares of Apple," Siri looks up the stock, but it will not place an order. That's because Siri cannot actually offer stock services or even advice. Apple definitely does not want Siri to be your stock advisor. We gave it a try, as you can see in Figure 2-9. Here are some examples of Siri queries that cause the assistant to complain. None of these produce the results you're looking for:

- Should I buy Apple?
- Siri, what are the 10 best picks on the New York Stock Exchange?
- Please pick me a good stock.

Using Wolfram Alpha

Wolfram Alpha is, according to Wikipedia, "an online service that answers factual queries directly by computing the answer from structured data, rather than providing a list of documents or web pages that might contain the answer as a search engine might."

Between Wikipedia and Wolfram Alpha, Apple has done an amazing job of opening up Siri searches to first-class information sources. Unlike Wikipedia queries, which open in the Safari browser, Wolfram Alpha answers are presented directly in the Siri interface. That makes it easy for you to keep going with a conversation, without having to hop into and out of Siri mode on your device (see Figure 2-10).

Figure 2-9
"What would I do? I'd shut it down and give the money back to the shareholders." (Michael Dell in 1997, answering a question about what could be done to fix the then-ailing Apple Computer, Inc.)

Figure 2-10
Use Wolfram Alpha queries to check definitions, look up information, calculate, and more.

When Siri recognizes a question that might be best answered or analyzed by Wolfram Alpha, it passes along your data and then displays whatever Wolfram Alpha returns. Siri uses this special view to present those results. They aren't verbally announced to you. Some of the questions you can get answers to seem incredible.

Querying Wolfram

Wolfram knows about quite a lot. The most reliable way to query Wolfram is to prefix your question with "Wolfram," "Ask Wolfram," or "What is." The "Wolfram" clue isn't strictly necessary, as you'll see in the following sample statements. Each of these statements is interpreted by Siri and then passed to Wolfram Alpha without explicitly using the word *Wolfram* at all.

- How many calories in a bagel?
- What does *repartee* mean?
- What is an 18 percent tip on $86.74 for four people?
- What's Morse code for *horse feathers*?
- Who's buried in Grant's tomb?
- How long do dogs live?
- What is the square root of 128?
- How many dollars is €45?
- What is the gossamer condor?
- What are the first 23 digits of *e*?
- How many dollars is ¥50,000?
- What was best picture in 1949?
- How many days until Easter?
- How many days between September 22, 1957 and today?
- How far away is Neptune?

- When is the next solar eclipse?
- What is the orbital period of Pluto?
- How far away is the sun?
- Show me the constellation of Ursa Major.
- What's the population of Montenegro?
- How high is Mt. Kilimanjaro?
- How deep is the Pacific Ocean?
- What's the price of diesel in Dubuque, Iowa?
- What's the price of lettuce in New York City?
- What's the integral of the cosine of x? (Siri and Wolfram Alpha seem to have problems with the sine function, confusing it with the word *sign*.)
- Graph $y = 9x^2 + 2$.
- What's the derivative of $3x^3 + 2x$?
- What's the boiling point of iron?
- What's the scientific name of a mountain lion?
- How many dimples are on a golf ball?
- How many episodes were there of *Buffy the Vampire Slayer*?
- What is the largest lake in the world?
- What is the longest filibuster?
- When did Colorado join the union?
- How many Earths fit inside the sun?
- How many turkeys are there in Turkey?
- What words contain *Steve*?
- What is the angle of the Leaning Tower of Pisa?
- How many people are there per pet fish in the United States?
- What's the atomic weight of lead?

Yes, Siri answers all these questions with the help of Wolfram Alpha and presents the results directly to you.

The depth of knowledge that Wolfram Alpha has is staggering. With Siri translating your questions into a format that Wolfram Alpha can understand, you have access to an incredible amount of information. Neither tool is perfect, and sometimes the way that Siri or Wolfram Alpha interprets your questions is amusing (to say the least), but both provide a huge amount of information and trivia.

 NOTE

Want to discover further interesting things to say to Wolfram Alpha? Follow @WolframFunFacts on Twitter. Wolfram regularly posts intriguing queries.

Wolfram Mode

At times, Siri goes into what we call Wolfram mode. To see this for yourself, say "Ask Wolfram" or "Wolfram" and then pause. From that point, Siri tries to get you to ask a question that it can look up for you on that website.

This is a great way to ensure that whatever you ask is sent to Wolfram Alpha for interpretation. You don't have to structure your question in any particular way or drop hints that you mean for Siri to redirect to Wolfram. Wolfram mode ensures that your questions go there directly.

If you enter this mode by accident, you can tell Siri, "Never mind." This throws you back to a normal Siri conversation.

The Wolfram Saving Throw

Try saying "igneous rock" to Siri on your iOS device. Siri does not know an answer, but it offers to perform a web search for you.

In this case, you might want to use what we call the Wolfram saving throw, which allows Wolfram to act as a superhero. Tap the microphone and say the magic phrase "Ask Wolfram."

Suddenly, bingo! Without any further work, Siri redirects your query to Wolfram Alpha—and saves the day. Figure 2-11 shows this maneuver in action.

Figure 2-11
The Wolfram saving throw converts a misunderstood phrase into a valid Wolfram Alpha search.

Wolfram Alpha Trick Lets You Know What Is Flying Overhead

Steve is a bit of an airline freak, so he loves looking up at the contrails of jets flying overhead and wondering where a plane

might be going. He recently found out that Wolfram Alpha can
tell you what airplanes are cruising around above you based on
your position and its knowledge of where various airline and
charter flights are located at any point in time. Because Siri has the
built-in capability to work with Wolfram Alpha, he thought he'd see
whether he could ask Siri to tell him about those flights overhead.

It took a few tries and some thought about what to ask Siri, but
he finally got it to work. Telling Siri "Ask Wolfram what flights
are overhead" produces the correct results. That query displays a
Wolfram Alpha output showing the flight or aircraft registration
number of flights that are currently visible from where you're
standing, their altitude, and the angle above the horizon. You see
this in the Figure 2-12 screenshots. You also get information on
what type of aircraft each is, how far away it is, and what direction
to look, as well as a sky map showing where the planes are.

Figure 2-12
Use Siri and Wolfram Alpha to determine which planes are flying above you.

Steve then made an attempt to coax details out of Siri about individual flights. He thought he would need to use the brains of Wolfram Alpha again, but he found that simply saying "Tell me about [name of airline] flight [flight number]" prompted Siri to display a web page showing the departure airport and time of the flight, along with the expected arrival airport, time, and gate.

The search isn't perfect, with flights between the West Coast and Asia showing up on the search despite the fact that there was no way the flights were flying over Colorado. But as with many of the tricks Siri can do, this feature shows the surprising depth of knowledge that you have access to by asking Siri.

Other Cool Stuff You Can Do with Wolfram Alpha

Here are several ways you can use Siri and Wolfram Alpha to do things you might not have thought of:

- **Generate a random number:** Tell Siri, "Tell me a random number" or "Pick a random number" or "What is a random number?" Wolfram Alpha returns a value between 0 and 1,000.

- **Generate a random password:** Tell Siri, "What is the password?" This generates a secure password for you.

- **Check earthquakes:** Tell Siri, "Wolfram, earthquakes," and let Siri find the most recent recorded earthquakes around the world.

- **Check upcoming holidays:** Say, "How many days until Thanksgiving?" This returns both the number of days and a helpful calendar so that you can chart the time until then.

- **Convert text to Morse code:** Say, "What is Morse code for *horsefeathers*?" You'll see the entire sequence laid out for your tapping pleasure.

- **Check your diet:** Say, "How many calories in a small apple?" Wolfram will tell you there are 75.

- **Ask out about time zones:** Say, "Wolfram, what is the local time in Jakarta?"

- **Look up nature facts:** Say, "Wolfram, what is the scientific name of a mountain lion?" It's puma concolor. Rabbits are leporidae, and peacocks are galliformes.

- **Query about your chances:** Say, "Wolfram, what is the probability of a full house?" For a random five-card hand, it's apparently 1 in 694.

- **Have fun with pop culture:** Say, "What is the airspeed velocity of an unladen swallow?" or "Wolfram, who shot the sheriff?"

- **Visualize colors:** If you work with colors, this can save you a lot of time. Say, "Wolfram pound sign E 9 7 4 5 1" (for burnt sienna/tangerine) or "Wolfram pound sign 2 9 A B 8 7" (for jungle green). This will also convert the colors to RGB values and look up closely matching house paint colors from Benjamin Moore. Be sure to scroll down to catch all the helpful information.

- **Graph equations:** Wolfram Alpha does great graphs and is ready to replace your expensive graphing calculator. Say, "Graph Y equals 4x plus 15," for example, or you can also try "What is c over lambda?" This latter is a cool graph, although we were hoping for "Nothing's nu with me. What's nu with you?"

Summary

Siri's powerful capabilities help you search for information through a quick, spoken conversation. In this chapter, you learned about the vast range of topics that Siri can respond to, by working with the built-in iOS apps, searching the Web, or passing information to an established search service such as Wikipedia or Wolfram Alpha. The points you want to remember from this chapter include the following:

- Siri offers a personal weather assistant, providing information on conditions either locally or on the other side of the world.

- Siri isn't limited to Google searches. Set your preferences to Google, Yahoo!, or Bing—or choose the search engine you prefer to use by saying its name during your request. It may feel odd to say, "Google this," "Bing that," or "Yahoo! whatever," but it helps Siri direct your request to the proper engine.

- Don't overlook Wikipedia. It provides another fabulous resource accessible from Siri.

- Enjoy up-to-the-moment sports info. Ask Siri about your favorite team, the score, and when the next game is due to start.

- Siri is your personal stock market reporter. It gives you up-to-date information on individual stocks, markets, and indices, as well as ratios and statistics.

- Wolfram Alpha's integration with Siri offers the most powerful information-gathering combinations on the iPhone 4S. From solving differential equations to telling you what planes are flying overhead, Siri and Wolfram Alpha transform incredible standalone tools into an unbeatable combo.

3

Using Siri to Stay in Touch

When it comes to contacts, Siri is the star of the show. It helps you stay in touch with others by supercharging your device's communication capabilities, letting you search for contacts, place phone calls, send text messages, and even compose email.

Siri understands relationships, too. Communication is all about relationships between people, and Siri can learn the established connections between you, your friends and co-workers, and your family. Tell Siri who is your dentist, your accountant, your hairdresser, and more. Then when you want to make an appointment, Siri will be ready to help retrieve that contact information.

Prepare to have some fun as you find out how Siri can act as your personal assistant when communicating with the world.

Contacts

When it comes to knowing who your contacts are, Siri provides a direct line into your iOS Contacts. For example, it's possible to look up phone numbers, email addresses, birthdays, and other data you would normally find in the device's Contacts list. You might ask:

- What's Victor's address?
- What is Dave Caolo's phone number?
- When is my wife's birthday?
- What is Joe's work address?
- Find people named Fred.
- Who's my hairdresser?
- Who is Jony Ive?
- Show Megan's home email address.

Each query looks up a specific detail for a given contact. Figure 3-1 shows a typical request, asking for the phone number for John Appleseed.

When Siri displays a contact, tap it to jump into the Contacts application to view or edit the entry.

Siri might at times have trouble distinguishing between contacts with similar names. If you ask, "What is John's phone number?", Siri asks you which John you mean. It does this by presenting a list of possible matches (see Figure 3-2). These matches ask the user to specify the intended contact.

Figure 3-1
Siri simplifies looking up specific contact
information.

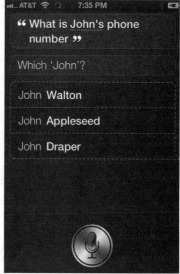

Figure 3-2
Siri might ask you to specify which contact
you mean when multiple entries match your
request.

To respond, tap a name or say the surname out loud—Siri
automatically listens whenever it asks you a clarification question.
After you've established the contact you desired, you can keep
referring to John. You won't have to answer any further questions.
"Send a text to John" uses the currently selected person's contact
information.

If you need to change the context from the current person to
another person of the same name, specify the full name (including
last name) in your request—for example, "Siri, what is John
Walton's phone number?" Siri always tries to remember context

to make each session as seamless as possible. In the case of the address book, the context is the most recently chosen contact.

 NOTE

> Nicknames are a great way to differentiate contacts, especially those with common names.

Searching for Contacts

Sometimes you want to view an entire contact entry. Siri helps you find contacts from your address book. For example, you might ask Siri, "Show Jason Russell" or "Who is Michael Manning?" Each of these queries locates a single person and displays the full contact information (see Figure 3-3).

Figure 3-3
You can view contacts by asking Siri to show them or by asking, "Who is . . . ?".

Once you see what contact information is available, you can easily use this data to send email, place phone calls, write texts, and more.

Creating Relationships

Relationships form an important part of the Siri/Contacts story. Although these elements have been part of the Address Book programming interface for many years, not until the introduction of Siri has adding relationships really made important sense on iOS. That's because Siri enables you to personalize your relationships with others and use those relationships as shortcuts when making requests.

You can say, "Mary Smith is my mother," or "John Appleseed is my friend" (see Figure 3-4) to establish those connections between your contact information and other entries in your address book.

Figure 3-4
Siri creates relationships to connect your contact information to others. You can edit those connections in the Contacts app.

Default relationships include mother, father, parent, sister, brother, child, friend, spouse, partner, manager, and assistant—but you are not limited to these. You can create any describable relationship for any recognized contact. For example, you might say, "Steven Sande is my hairdresser," or "Megan Lavey-Heaton is my favorite cartoon author." Siri adds those relationships to your contacts, as you can see in Figure 3-4.

Relationships can be made with only known contacts. If you use an unknown person—for example, "Benjamin Franklin is my tennis partner"—Siri complains (in this case, "There's no one in your contacts matching 'Benjamin Franklin'")

 NOTE

Historically, Siri has had problems properly supporting relationships for Exchange and Gmail address books. Be aware that you, too, might experience some problems.

Here are some examples of relationships you can establish with Siri:

- My mom is Susan Islington.
- Michael Fredericks is my brother.
- Call my sister at work.
- Text my assistant.
- Call my hairdresser.
- Billy Appleseed is my spouse.
- Steve Sande is my friend.
- Fran Yeddis is my realtor.
- When is my husband's birthday?
- Emma Sadun is my child.

Each relationship is stored in the standard Contacts application. You can edit any inadvertent relationships you might have added by mistake (for example, "Justin Bieber is my boyfriend"—yeah, right, smart-aleck daughter who swiped the iPhone).

Creating an Alternative Identity for Yourself

Perhaps you've heard this joke: You tell Siri, "Call me an ambulance," and Siri responds, "From now on, I'll call you, 'An Ambulance.' Okay?" Leanna Lofte pointed out in a great write-up at iMore (http://imore.com) that this joke is actually of practical use.

It's possible to create a more intimate identity for yourself by telling Siri to call you by your nickname—or indulge your monomaniacal streak by instructing it to call you "master" or "emperor" (see Figure 3-5, top). Check on your current nickname by asking Siri, "Who am I?" (see Figure 3-5, bottom).

Siri does this by checking two fields in your primary Contacts entry. The Nickname field takes priority. When you say, "Call me [followed by some name]," Siri updates your Nickname field. Another way to establish an alternative name without adding a nickname to your entry is to use the phonetic guides.

The Phonetic First Name and Phonetic Last Name fields have been around for quite some time in the Address Book application on both iOS and OS X. They help you pronounce people's names when calling them. For example, you might enter "Ser Hee Yo" for a contact named Sergio, referring to that pronunciation as you're placing your call. (You can also add free-form notes in each contact for other cultural hints.) Siri now uses those fields to override the default pronunciation of your name as well.

To add these fields in iOS, tap Edit, scroll down to Add Field, and then choose one of the phonetic options.

Figure 3-5
Siri can assign your nickname on demand. Check that nickname by asking, "Who am I?"

Pronouncing Your Name

If Siri doesn't seem to pronounce your name the way it should, use these same phonetic fields to give it speaking hints. Enter your name the way it should sound ("Sandy" instead of "Sande," for example); this gives Siri the information it needs to address you correctly.

You can save some time by speaking the proper pronunciation into the field. This works great if your name is Sande. It works less great if your name is Sadun (proper pronunciation in America is *suh'Doon* and in Italy is *SAAAH-doon*).

If your name does not break down into common English words, you'll end up with nonsense or nothing at all in that field. Just type the name, and help Siri know exactly how to say your name.

Placing Phone Calls with Siri

Siri uses your address book contact information to simplify the way you place phone calls. For example, you might say one of the following phrases to initiate a call with one of your personal contacts. If a person is not listed in your address book, explicitly speak the number.

- Call Jason.
- Call Biffster. (Yes, Siri works with nicknames, too.)
- Call Jennifer Wright mobile.
- Call Susan on her work phone.
- Call 408-555-1212.
- Call home.
- FaceTime Lisa.

Be aware that Siri does not confirm phone calls before placing them (see Figure 3-6, left). It initiates the call directly and immediately switches to the phone (or FaceTime) application. You can cancel a call as needed, but you use an airtime minute in the process. Alternatively, press the Home button before control passes to the Phone application.

When contacts offer several phone numbers, you can help Siri by specifying which number to use. For example, you might say, "Call John Appleseed at work," or "Call John Appleseed at home." If Siri cannot exactly match your request to a given number, it tries to offer you an alternative.

Figure 3-6
Siri places calls directly without requiring confirmation (left). If Siri cannot match the destination phone to a contact number (for example, you asked to call home, but there's no home number), it tries to use another number instead (right).

In Figure 3-6 (right), John Appleseed's contact entry contains just one phone number, and it's labeled as Work. If you ask to call him at home, Siri suggests the work number as an alternative. You can confirm using the work number or cancel by pressing the Home button.

Text Messages

The Siri voice assistant helps you use your voice to check your messages, send a reply, and start new conversations. With Siri, you can perform many of your iMessage tasks from anywhere on your iOS device.

Siri supports sending or receiving three different types of messages—standard SMS text messages, MMS multimedia (pictures and video) messages, and Apple's new iMessage format. iMessage bypasses the traditional phone-based messaging system and instead transfers text and multimedia messages over the Internet.

Like the proverbial honey badger, Siri really doesn't care how the messages are sent. It chooses the correct transport method and ensures that your message is properly dictated and sent to the recipient. One nice feature of iMessage is that it lets you know when the message has been delivered and also shows you if someone is in the process of typing a reply.

Reading Texts

Siri loves to read your new text messages to you. This is very useful if you're out walking or running and receive a message you want to hear. How do you do it? Just ask!

When a new message arrives, tell Siri, "Read my new message." If you want it repeated, tell Siri, "Read it again." Siri fills you in on all your new messages while keeping your hands free for other tasks. You can also ask, "Do I have any new messages?," in case you've lost track.

You reply to your messages in a variety of ways. When you listen to a message, Siri follows along. This context enables you to say, "Reply, 'That's great news,'" or "Tell him I'll be there in a few minutes." If the matter is urgent, just say, "Call her," and Siri uses the contact information associated with the message you just received to look up the user's phone number.

Replying to Texts

After Siri reads the message, you can reply to the message hands free. This is perfect when you need to respond to an urgent message while driving. Here's what you need to say to Siri:

- Reply, "That's great news."
- Tell him I'll be there in 10 minutes.
- Call her.

Sending Messages

Siri listens for some keywords before sending a text message—*tell*, *send a message*, or *text*—although there might be other terms that it understands. Figure 3-7 shows an example of a message going to Erica.

To create a message, instruct Siri to tell someone something, such as, "Tell Steve, I'll be right there." You can also "text" or "send a message." For example, you can say, "Send a message to Mike saying 'How about tomorrow?'" or, "Text Anthony 'Where are you? I have been waiting for 20 minutes.'" Here are some common phrases to use when telling Siri to dictate and send a message to someone:

- Tell Megan "I'll be right there."
- Send a message to Dave Caolo.
- Text Steve and Megs that I'll be a little late.
- Send a message to Paige saying, "How about tomorrow?"
- Tell Cathy the birthday present was great.
- Send a message to Susan on her mobile saying I'll feed the dog.
- Send a message to 408-555-1212.
- Text Mike and Victor "Where are you?"

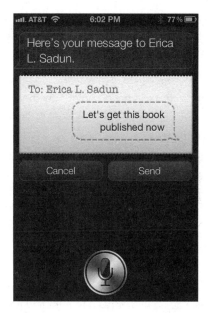

Figure 3-7
When you have an urgent message you need to send to someone, Siri writes it for you and then asks if you want to send it.

Notice that if you don't have a contact for a person you want to message, but you do have a mobile number, you can tell Siri to send a message to that number. For example, say, "Send a message to 408-555-1212," and Siri prompts you for the text contents. Then speak your message.

Confirming Messages

When Siri asks you to confirm what you said, you reply by asking it to read the message back to you. (Say, "Read it to me," "Read it back to me," "Review," or "Read it again.") You can also verbally correct text or mail messages you have composed. The following examples let Siri know that you're not satisfied with what you've said. Notice that it is possible to change the contents completely or add new material:

- Change it to, "Let's meet at 3:00 p.m."
- Add, "Can't wait, exclamation point." (By the way, you can do this even if Siri doesn't mention it as an option.)
- No, send it to Megs.
- No. (This keeps the message without sending it.)
- Cancel. (This cancels the message entirely.)

When you are satisfied with your text or email message, say something like, "Yes, send it," to start the delivery of the message.

Mail

Siri offers a totally new way of sending and reading email and text messages. You no longer need to hunt and peck on the iOS keyboard to assemble your written communications. Simply speak to Siri to create emails with your voice.

Creating Mail

The proper way to ask Siri to create a new mail message addressed to someone in your Contacts list, as well as add a subject to that message, is to say, "Email [name or nickname] about [subject]" or just "Email [name or nickname]." Telling Siri, "Email Erica about book cover," produces the following conversation (see Figure 3-8).

At this point, Siri asks what you want the email to say. This enables the dictation function, and Siri listens attentively as you speak your email.

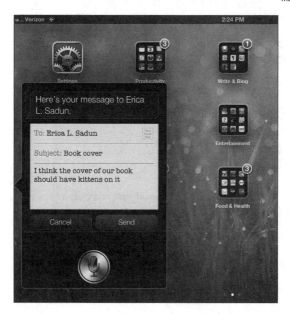

Figure 3-8
Part of a conversation with Siri to write and send an email. The cover of this book might or might not have kittens on it.

For contacts who don't have a nickname, use their first or first and last names (for example, Erica or Erica Sadun) to find the email address. If you have more than one email address for a person, Siri prompts you to select one.

You can shortcut the question/response process when creating an email by telling Siri, "Mail contact about subject and say 'Message.'" As an example, you can say, "Mail Mom and Dad about Barb's hospital stay and say, 'Thank you for sending the flowers, period, they were lovely, exclamation point.'" That seemingly rambling comment creates a ready-to-send message that looks like the one shown in Figure 3-9.

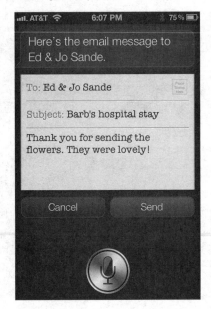

Figure 3-9
This email was addressed, given a subject, and written all with one long phrase directed at Siri.

When dictating email, don't feel that you have to do it all at once.
If you're more comfortable being prompted for a subject and then
content, go ahead and do things that way. Siri helps you create
messages in the way that best fits your personal style.

 NOTE

Don't forget that you can dictate punctuation (period,
exclamation point, question mark) and line breaks (new
paragraph and new line). These small touches help make your
emails and texts more user-friendly.

Checking Mail

Siri is not a one-trick pony when it comes to working with the Mail app. It can also check your incoming mail and display it on your iOS screen (although it cannot read it to you aloud). Siri tells you how many emails you have ("Okay, Erica, I found at least 25 emails"), but little more than that.

Here are some email-related phrases you can try with Siri:

- Check email.
- Any new email from Kelly today?
- Show new mail about the wedding.
- Show the email from Nik yesterday.

Siri responds to any request to delete emails with a terse "I'm not allowed to delete emails for you" message. As we discussed earlier in this book, Siri focuses more on content creation than management. Apple probably made this a conscious design choice to prevent possible disasters from a misspoken word.

Responding to Mail

When reading an email message, responding to it with Siri can take several forms. To send a Mail response, say something like, "Reply, 'Dear Mom, thanks for sending the flowers to the hospital.'" Want to call the person who sent you email? Just say, "Call [him/her/name] at [work/home/iPhone]." Siri dials the phone number, and within seconds, you're responding in person to the message.

Social Networking

Siri now does social networking. Starting in iOS 6, Siri integrates with Facebook and Twitter, letting you post updates to your favorite networks with just a few spoken words. With Siri, you can now say:

- Post to Facebook "Headed to the new Pixar movie."
- Write on my Wall "Just landed in San Jose!"
- Post to Twitter "Another beautiful day in Cupertino."
- Tweet with my location "Great concert."
- Tweet "Meeting up with Brian Conway for lunch today."
- Tweet "The new iPad looks insanely great!" hashtag Apple Keynote.

Figure 3-10 shows how you can create a Tweet using your voice. Simply tell Siri to tweet or post to Twitter, and your message will soon be on its way.

Both Facebook and Twitter rely on you having entered your credentials in Settings. Go to Settings > Facebook and Settings > Twitter to add accounts.

You can launch the Twitter app (if installed) by saying, "Check my tweets." This leaves Siri and moves to the standalone app. Similarly, you can say, "Open Facebook." You cannot, however, check your Wall or your timeline from Siri.

Friends

Find My Friends is a utility that you can download from the App Store. This app gives any approved contacts your current location. Likewise, you can ask your friends with iOS units for access to their locations. Siri and Find My Friends make it easy to find out where your friends and relatives are at any given point and time.

To find a contact, you don't need to launch Find My Friends. Just ask Siri, and it tells you the location of a particular person or group by displaying a map (see Figure 3-11).

ericasadun @ericasadun
Posting to Twitter with Siri is lots of fun!
Collapse ← Reply 🗑 Delete ★ Favorite

Figure 3-10
You can post Twitter and Facebook updates from within Siri.

Figure 3-11
Friends who have given you permission to know their location and who have their iOS devices turned on can be located with a single Siri command.

You can use quite a few Siri phrases to check the whereabouts of your buddies. Here are some examples that demonstrate friend-finding capabilities:

- Where's Jason? (Useful to know, especially if Jason wears a hockey mask or if you're supposed to meet him for lunch and he's running 15 minutes late. Seeing that Jason is still driving down the interstate is a major clue that he might have hit some traffic.)

- Where is my sister? (You can use relationship names with Find My Friends, just as you do for making phone calls or texting.)

- Is my husband at home? (If so, don't bring your boyfriend home with you!)

- Where are all my friends? (If they're running away from you, you might want to cut down on all that garlic.)

- Who is here? (We can't wait to use that when we're at Macworld/iWorld, or anywhere else where we can catch up with Internet buddies we might not have met in person.)

- Who is near me?

Siri won't know where your friends are if you haven't first set them up with Find My Friends. Use the app to send invitations to your closest friends and relatives using iPhone, iPod Touch, or iPad.

Also be aware you need to log in to Find My Friends to use the service with Siri. When you do, you'll be authorized for a long period of time. If you try to use your device while driving and immediately expect to find people, you might be disappointed. Always be sure to log in before heading to the car if you expect to use this feature.

Summary

Your iOS device and Siri are better communicators than those units from *Star Trek*. Sure, your device isn't as small as those cool badges on the later generations of *Star Trek*, but not only can your phone call someone at your voice command, but you can send text messages and emails as well. Plus, you won't get bruises from hitting your chest all the time. Throw in FaceTime, Facebook, or Twitter, and you have an extremely powerful communication tool.

You should take away the following points from this chapter:

- Relationships, especially unique ones, simplify your life when using Siri. If your spouse has a common name such as John or Barbara or Steve, referring to him or her as "my wife" or "my husband" helps jump past the hurdles of figuring out which John, Barbara, or Steve you are referencing. Take advantage of relationships to speed up texts, emails, and calls to important people in your life.

- The Contacts app provides tight Siri integration. Information about a contact's phone numbers, addresses, email addresses, and more is just a question away.

- Twitter and Facebook integration is fun and useful. It's a lot easier to ask Siri to post an update for you than to sit and type it in yourself. Share the moment while you're having the moment—don't pull yourself away just so you can hunt and peck on the iOS keyboard.

- Use Siri voice commands for calling, emailing, and texting your contacts. For email and texts, use the dictation commands from later in this book to create complete messages with proper punctuation. You can dictate and send texts and email messages with just your voice.

- Siri reads your incoming text messages to you but cannot read full email messages. This is a feature we're looking forward to in future Siri updates. To reply to a message, just tell Siri to answer it and then dictate your reply.

4

Talking to Your Day-Timer

For many people, iOS replaces handwritten organizers like the classic Day-Timer. If you're too young to be familiar with Day-Timers, they had printed pages with spaces for reminders, notes, and calendar appointments, as well as lists of contacts. They cost more than they were really worth and weighed more than an iPad—and we *loved* them. Ridiculously.

Instead of scrawling handwritten notes onto printed calendar pages, iOS and Siri set up appointments, take notes, and set reminders through simple conversations. This process feels more like having your own personal assistant taking care of business for you than using an electronic device.

This chapter introduces you to the ways you can use Siri to help schedule and organize your life. It's time to throw away that handwritten organizer.

Calendars

If you're familiar with iOS, you might already be a fan of the
Calendar app for keeping track of your appointments and
meetings. With Siri, you have your own concierge at your beck
and call, handling all your Calendar events. And through the
magic of iCloud, any Calendar events you make with Siri are
immediately synchronized to any other devices you might have
connected to the service.

Adding Events

Adding an event using Siri follows a standard conversational
pattern. You tell it, "Set up a meeting," "Meet with someone,"
"Schedule a meeting," or "Make an appointment." You specify
whom the meeting is with and when it takes place. Figure 4-1
shows this approach in action. You might say:

- Set up a meeting with Jimmy at 7.
- Schedule my dental appointment. (Using the word schedule is
  a great way to tell Siri to work with the Calendar.)
- Meet with Emily at noon.
- Set up a meeting about hiring tomorrow at 9 a.m.
- New appointment with Susan Park Friday at 3.
- Schedule a planning meeting at 8:30 today in the boardroom.

Many times when setting up a meeting, you want your device
to alert you a few minutes before it starts. Reminders help you
remember to participate. Unfortunately, there doesn't appear to
be a way at this time to tell Siri to add an alert to a calendar event.
To add an alert and specify the sound to use when the alert is
made, you need to use reminders, which you read about in the
next section. Reminders play an alert tone by default.

Figure 4-1
Asking Siri to schedule a meeting creates a calendar entry with all the pertinent information filled in. You specify who, what, where, and when for these events.

You might want to create a calendar event for a meeting to block out time on your calendar and send invitations to others, and then make a reminder to alert you before the start of the meeting.

Making Changes

In real life, meetings and appointments may shift. That's fine; Siri is amenable to change. Here are some phrases you might use to update an event on your calendar:

- Move my 10 a.m. meeting to 2:30. (Siri will know the meeting is for 2:30 p.m.)

- Reschedule my appointment with Dr. Hathaway to next Monday at 9 a.m.

- Add Erica to my meeting with Apple.

- Cancel the final book review meeting.

- Change the location of my 3 p.m. meeting tomorrow to Bob's office.

These phrases let Siri know that you're modifying existing events rather than creating new ones in your calendar.

 NOTE

Siri uses your contacts information to figure out how to match location names (such as *home* and *office*) with contact names (such as Bob and Jennifer). Bob's work address in Contacts helps locate "Bob's office." Make sure you allow Siri to use location-based services. In Settings > Location Services, set the switch for Siri to On.

Checking Your Calendar

Many times you just want to find out something about a meeting, such as what time and date it's set for, where the meeting is, or what you've got scheduled for a specific day. Never fear, Siri's here! A quick conversation with Siri is like asking a human assistant to look at your calendar for you (see Figure 4-2).

Calendar Queries

What kind of calendar-related questions can you ask Siri? Here are several examples of statements you might use to ask Siri about upcoming events on your calendar:

- What does the rest of my day look like?

- What's on my calendar for Wednesday?

- When is my next appointment?
- When am I meeting with Erica?
- Where is my next meeting?

Figure 4-2
Need to know what's coming up on your agenda for tomorrow? Ask Siri, and you get an immediate answer.

When your meeting doesn't have a location, Siri tells you that it doesn't know where the meeting is to be held. Siri's pretty smart, so it also responds with an "I don't think you have any meetings with [whomever]" when you mistakenly think you've set up a meeting with someone.

Siri can also tell you the date for an upcoming or past day of the week. For example, if you ask, "What date was last Thursday?", Siri responds with an answer such as, "It was Thursday, October 13, 2012." Even more impressive, you can ask, "What day of the week was December 7, 1941?" (or any other date), and you'll get an answer.

Reminders

Reminders are different from calendar events. Calendars mark your appointments; reminders tell you what you have to do. Think of reminders, which are accessed through the iOS Reminders app, as an intelligent to-do list.

Reminders can be time and location sensitive. They often have a schedule associated with them (think of this as a deadline for completing a task). You can also use the GPS features of your device in a feature called geofencing. Geofencing reminds you of something when you arrive at or leave a location.

Figure 4-3 shows a conversation with Siri to set up a time-based reminder—in this case, to help you remember to take your medicine. Siri sets up a new reminder and uses the task you specified—namely, "Take my pills"—to create a little prompt at a time you specified ("9 a.m. tomorrow").

To ask for a reminder when you arrive at or leave a destination, you tell Siri "when I leave here" or "when I get home." Siri can remind you when you leave or arrive "here" or at home, work, school, or gym—both yours and someone else's.

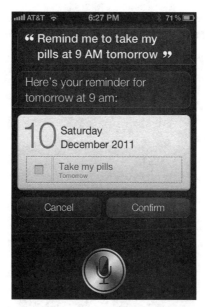

Figure 4-3
This phrase tells Siri to remind you to take needed medicines tomorrow morning. Humans are notoriously forgetful. Siri isn't.

Figure 4-4 shows how to ask Siri for a reminder about milk when arriving at Albertsons, a local Denver grocery store. Siri can act a little fussy when it comes to arbitrary locations like this. To make this work reliably, Erica created a custom contact named "Albertsons Albertsons" with a company name of, you guessed it, "Albertsons", along with the actual physical address.

This "department of redundancy department" style showcases how you should always test your contacts and reminders scenarios instead of depending on them to work exactly the way you intended. You might need to do some tweaking to ensure that recognition works exactly the way you intended, especially for business locations without normal first and last names.

Figure 4-4
Siri can create location-based reminders. Make sure you set up a recognizable contact with the location information. Although redundant, adding the destination name to the contact's first name, last name, and company name helps Siri better recognize the locations of businesses.

How Siri Can Remind You

Siri is great at remembering. Even when human memory fails, Siri keeps track of things you've long since forgotten you had to do. Here are examples of some of the other things you can say to Siri to have it remind you:

- Remind me to call Mom.
- Remind me to text Jake when I get home.

- Remember to take an umbrella.
- Remind me to take my medicine at 6 a.m. tomorrow.
- Remind me to find an ATM when I leave here.
- Remind me when I leave to call Jason.
- Remind me to finish the report by 6 p.m.
- Remind me to park outside when I arrive at Bob's house.
- Remind me to buy milk every 4 days.
- Remind me to join the conference call every Wednesday at 3 p.m.

The last two conversations set up recurring reminders. You can ask Siri to remind you every day, every week, every two weeks, once a month, or once a year. Now there's no excuse for forgetting your anniversary, guys!

A Word of Caution

One word of caution when using the GPS-based reminders: Doing so enables Location Services for the Reminders app. A small white arrow on the iOS status bar next to the battery indicator means that your device is actively finding your current location.

Why should you be concerned? Location Services is notorious for causing higher-than-average power use, resulting in shorter-than-expected battery life. The reminders are great; the diminished battery charge might not be. Use these features with the understanding that they might affect your battery charge-to-charge.

To use geofencing, make sure you have properly enabled Siri in Settings. Check Settings > Privacy > Location Services (which must be On) > Siri (which also must be On).

Creating Notes

Siri makes it easy to add quick hands-free notes on iOS. You can't beat the convenience of getting tiny tidbits of information recorded with a single tap and chat. With Siri, you can record information as you think of it. No need to wait until you arrive at the office or get to a coffee shop to sit down. This section covers additional ways you can use this handy feature.

Creating Single-Item Notes

It's easy to add single-item notes such as "Note that I spent $5 on parking" (see Figure 4-5) or "Note: Check out that new Parry Grip compilation album." Each of these spoken commands creates a single standalone note item in the Notes application.

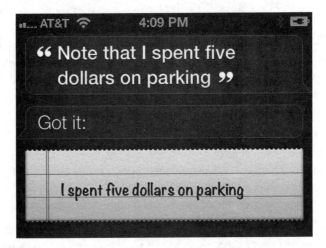

Figure 4-5
Siri easily creates single-item notes for you when you're on the go. Tell it what you need to remember, and let Siri keep track of the information.

Adding Items to the Current Note

Siri retains context, so you can add items to the currently edited note one at a time. The key word here is *add*. For example, say "Add 'Do laundry,'" and Siri adds "Do laundry" to the current note. Alternatively, say "Add" or "Add to note." Siri responds, "What would you like to add?" and automatically starts listening for a response. Each time, you add one item to the current note, so you expand the note as needed. Figure 4-6 shows how to create and then add to a note.

Figure 4-6
Use "add" commands to add items to the current note.

Starting New Notes

When you want to begin a new note instead of add to an existing one, just tell Siri, "Take a note" or "Start a note"—or just use the one-sentence "Note that… something…" structure.

If you don't provide contents, Siri responds with "OK, I can take that note for you… just tell me what you want it to say." You then use "Add" to keep adding to that new note.

Naming Notes

To name notes, refer to the first item added to them. For example, you can say, "Create a 'do this' note," and then add notes to that by saying, "Add 'Buy milk' to my 'do this' note" or just "Add 'Buy milk.'" Figure 4-7 shows an example of using a named list to add items.

Figure 4-7
Creating and adding notes. Tap on any note to view it in the Notes application.

Finding Notes

Retrieve the note by asking Siri to find it. Figure 4-8 shows the response of "Find my 'do this' note." Unfortunately, you cannot ask Siri, "Read it to me"; currently, Siri reads only incoming text messages. Instead, Siri displays the note it finds on the screen for your reading pleasure.

Figure 4-8
Siri retrieves notes by title, which corresponds to the first line

Siri allows you to search for notes by date as well as title. Say, "Show me my notes from today" or "Show my notes from May 22," and Siri will oblige.

Telling Siri "Show me my notes" or "Show me all the notes" displays all your notes as a table of contents. Tap any of the notes to open it in the iOS Notes application.

NOTE

Unfortunately, Siri does not offer any note-editing features other than adding items. You cannot delete notes without going into the Notes application.

Clock Functions

Siri is nicely integrated with iOS clock functions. The usual clock functions built into the device firmware include an alarm clock, a countdown timer, a world clock displaying the current time in locations around the globe, and a stopwatch. Siri doesn't want to be a stopwatch when it grows up, but it happily serves you in the other clock functions.

Alarms

When you're trying to set an alarm clock, usually you press the little button and watch the wake time spin past, and then you have to do it all over again. It's easier on iOS; you just spin the hour and minute you want to wake up to set an alarm.

As expected, Siri makes setting an alarm a matter of talking to your device and telling it when you want that alarm to go off. Figure 4-9 shows an extreme example of a conversation with Siri asking it to wake you the next morning.

Here are some examples of how you can ask Siri to handle alarms:

- Wake me up tomorrow at 7 a.m.
- Set an alarm for 6:30 a.m.
- Wake me up in 8 hours.
- Delete all alarms.

- Turn morning alarms off/on. (Turns all alarms off or on at once.)
- Change my 6:30 alarm to 6:45.
- Turn off my 6:30 alarm.
- Cancel my 7:15 a.m. alarm. ("Okay, I deleted your 7:15 a.m. alarm. Now we can all get some sleep.")
- Delete my 7:30 alarm.

Figure 4-9
Siri understands the "wake me up at 9 a.m. tomorrow" part and sets an alarm. The brilliant and friendly Siri totally ignores the "whoa, dude."

How do you know what sound iOS will use to wake you from your sweet dreams? It uses whatever alarm tone you used previously, or you can tap on the Alarm button of the Clock app, tap the Edit button, and then select a sound.

Sadly, Siri doesn't come with a snooze command—it won't listen as you plead for "just 10 more minutes" of sleep (see Figure 4-10). Perhaps a future version of Siri will provide that capability.

Figure 4-10
Siri doesn't exactly "get" the concept of snoozing. You'll have to open your eyes and tap the Snooze button instead.

 NOTE

In iOS 6, you can select any song as your alarm tone, not just Apple-supplied sound samples.

Checking the Clock

When it comes to the world clock functions of Siri, you can start with your little part of the world. Siri knows where you are and responds to a query of "What time is it?" by telling you the local time.

This is a bit pointless because every single Siri screen displays the time for you, but this allows Siri to speak the time—handy when you're driving or otherwise don't want to move your eyes. You can also ask, "What's today's date?" or "What year is it?"

That's the least of its capabilities, however. When you need to know whether it's a good time to call your business partner in Mumbai, all you need to do is ask what time it is there (see Figure 4-11). Instantly, Siri gives you a time that translates both the actual hour and the date. In this example, it's already tomorrow in Mumbai.

You can ask:

- What's the time?
- What time is it in Cupertino, California?
- What is today's date?
- How many days until Christmas?
- What's the date this Saturday?

Using a Timer

Our families love to grill, and one of the key success factors we've discovered in our outdoor cooking is to use a timer to let us know when to flip the food, take meat off the heat, or let it rest.

Since Siri has entered our lives, we can now set a timer one-handed. Press the Home button (or bring an iPhone to your ear) and say, "Set a timer for 7 minutes." You quickly get verification from Siri that the timer is counting down.

Figure 4-11
The world clock capabilities of Siri enable you to determine the time for most major cities around the world.

You can also pause, resume, or stop timers. Here are examples of using Siri to set timers:

- Set the timer for 10 minutes.
- Show the timer.
- Pause the timer.
- Resume.
- Stop it.
- Reset the timer.

Siri uses whatever timer alert sound you've set under the Timer tab of the Clock app. You select your favorite ear-shattering noise by tapping the When Timer Ends button. If you want to know how much longer the timer has to go, just ask Siri, "What's the timer status?"

Siri must have taken cooking lessons at some point because it is aware of how long it takes to cook an egg. Setting a 3-minute timer often results in Siri replying, "Don't overcook that egg!"

Summary

With Siri working overtime on iOS, it's like having a personal assistant who works for you wherever and whenever you want. Through easy, natural-language statements, Siri sets appointments, checks your calendar, and sets and announces reminders.

Siri is also an incredible help with time functions. Whether you need to set an alarm to wake yourself up, set a duration timer for cooking, or find the correct time anywhere in the world, a quick conversation gets the job done. Here are some points to take away from this chapter:

- Adding an appointment to your calendar represents just one task Siri performs. Remember that you can work with Siri to get your next appointment; determine what your calendar looks like for a certain day; and change meeting attendees, times, and locations through verbal commands.

- Reminders are different from appointments, in that they are more like a to-do list that can have a deadline. You can also set Siri to remind you of something when you arrive at or leave somewhere using geofencing features. Your device monitors your location and triggers those reminders when you approach or leave a tagged destination.

- This chapter introduced a lot of great reminder tips, but there's a lot more you can do with them. Move on to the next chapter to see how you can integrate reminders with your shopping lists.

- People who like to annotate their lives with handwritten Post-it Notes will love Siri's capability to create and add to lists through speech. Imagine dictating a shopping list to your iOS device as you drive to a store, and you have a good idea of the power of Siri's interactions with notes.

- Interacting with the iOS clock no longer requires hands-on action. Instead, ask Siri to set, change, or delete an alarm; start or stop a timer; or tell you what time it is in any major city of the world.

5

Going Shopping with Siri

In our busy twenty-first-century lives, time is a precious commodity. Siri helps you make the best of your limited free time. It helps you search for goods, services, and entertainment; find your way to local businesses; and even calculate tips and taxes.

This chapter explores the ways Siri works at your command to make your shopping journeys as smooth as possible. Siri hunts down the items you crave and reminds you to buy something when you are near a store that carries that item.

In your pocket, Siri is an invisible assistant. It gets you out of stores and back to enjoying friends, family, and your precious free time.

Products and Services

Siri hunts down products and services at your command. You might say to Siri, "I'm hungry," or "I'm in the mood for Italian food," and Siri tries to find exactly what you're looking for based on your current location (see Figure 5-1).

Siri replies to your requests by matching local business to your statement. In the case of "I'm hungry," it lists nearby restaurants, enabling you to preview all the options. Just tap any of the offerings to find directions, phone numbers, and reviews.

Figure 5-1
Siri finds restaurants, stores, services, and more, all with simple queries.

Siri is happy to assist, no matter what kind of goods or services you desire. It handles a wide range of shopping requests. The following statements demonstrate how you might start a local search-based conversation with Siri:

- Find me a bike shop.
- Where can I go to read a book?
- I'm looking for a health clinic.
- What's a good place for dinner?
- Is there a dentist near me?
- How far is it from here to a library?
- I want to buy clothing.
- Find me a Honda dealer.
- Where can I get gas for my car?
- Is there a train station near here?
- I need a drug store.
- Where can I find a basketball?
- Where can I buy milk?

When you ask a qualitative question, Siri orders items by ratings. For example, you might ask, "What's a good place to buy clothes?" or "What's the best bike shop?" It uses Yelp ratings to differentiate which locations are better reviewed and which are less well received.

Tap the star ratings next to each vendor to open the Yelp app (if installed) and read the customer reviews. This integration helps you evaluate whether it is the right place for you. If you haven't already installed Yelp, what are you waiting for? It's one of the best shopping and eating apps on your iPhone or other iOS device.

Sorting is always set up to simplify the task you've asked of Siri, whether it's related to distance, rating, or price. If you ask a general question, Siri's searches show closer items first, as in Figure 5-1. If you ask, "What's an inexpensive place to eat?", Siri sorts by price. Your question helps fine-tune Siri's response. Here's how you might want to set up your question to control the sorting of your results:

- **Where is/Find me/Show me nearby:** sorts by distance
- **What's the best/Where are good:** sorts by ratings
- **What's an inexpensive/Find me a fancy:** sorts by price

Checking Prices

Not sure whether you're getting a bargain or being ripped off? Siri can look up regional pricing for basic commodities, such as gasoline, bread, potatoes, ground beef, butter, eggs, orange juice, sugar, and milk. You can also look at average prices of toothpaste, facial tissues, shampoo, detergent, dry cleaning, haircuts, movie tickets, newspapers, and bowling, among other standard items.

For example, you might ask Siri, "What is the average price of a gallon of gasoline in Denver?" (see Figure 5-2) or "How much does milk cost in Denver?" That $3.50 gallon of gasoline might actually start to sound like a bargain. In addition to pricing in big cities, Siri provides prices based on a state or national level.

Siri cannot look up shelf prices at the local grocery store—you only get averages. Siri also won't look for vendors based on pricing, so you cannot ask, "Where is the cheapest gas station near me?" or "Where can I find inexpensive groceries?" Siri will reply, "I can't look specifically for price range…my apologies."

Figure 5-2
$3.76 a gallon? Ouch! Siri enables you to check average prices on many commodities.

Shopping Math

Siri offers great tools when it comes to comparison shopping and calculating specific values. For example, you can check the sales tax, convert currencies, or split a bill. Here are some scenarios where Siri brings math skills to day-to-day shopping.

Adding Sales Tax

Siri calculates sales tax through your spoken requests. Just ask how much a purchase is with tax added for a given city, as shown in Figure 5-3. This is a great way to calculate your final purchase price. If you omit the city name, Siri tries to guess your location and replies appropriately.

Figure 5-3
Siri adds sales tax.

Calculating Tips

Get some great service at lunch? You might want to consider a generous tip. Siri helps with that, too! As Figure 5-4 shows, Siri calculates the total of your bill with tip. If you try this on a member of the iPhone family (as opposed to the iPad), be sure to scroll down. Page through the results to see the amount with the tip you requested, as well as the amount with standard tip values such as 10%, 15%, 20%, and 25%.

Siri can also split bills. Ask Siri, "What is an 18% tip on $86.74 for four people?" and it returns the display shown in Figure 5-4 (right). That's about $26 per person, for a total check of $102.35—or $104 rounded up. Again, make sure to scroll down for further details.

Figure 5-4
Siri is also a tipping genius. Left: "What is $4.22 with a 20% tip?" Right: "What is an 18% tip on $86.74 for four people?"

Currency Conversion

If you are traveling abroad or purchasing from merchants overseas, Siri is there to help. As Figure 5-5 shows, Siri converts currencies to show you what a purchase in British pounds would cost in U.S. dollars.

This figure does not, of course, include any extra fees that the vendor might charge for conversion when shopping in dollars or that your credit card company might charge when shopping in local currency. Always keep in mind fees incurred when shopping with various forms of tender. Many credit card issuers charge currency conversion fees for foreign purchases made with their credit, debit, and check cards, as well as any ATM cash withdrawals.

Figure 5-5
Converting between currencies helps you shop abroad or from foreign websites.

Monetary exchange rates vary on a daily basis. Siri's conversion calculations are meant to give you an approximate sense of value—how much that item might cost in Rupees or Euros as opposed to dollars. Don't depend on these numbers to be exact; they reflect only the current quoted conversion rates.

Preparing a Shopping List

Cliff Joyce of Pure Blend Software introduced us to our favorite way of putting together shopping lists in Siri: Start in the Reminders application and create a new list. To do this, tap the Lists button at the top-left corner of the application (it looks like three lines on top of each other). Tap Edit, tap Create New List, and enter the name Groceries. Finally, click Done. After you have a list named Groceries (see Figure 5-6), you can refer to it in Siri.

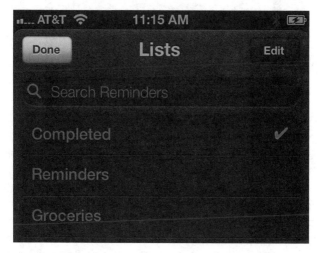

Figure 5-6
When you create lists in the Reminders app, you can refer to them by name in Siri.

After you create the list, you can add new items at any time with simple requests. For example, tell Siri, "Add eggs to my Groceries list." Siri asks you to confirm the new item (see Figure 5-7). Say, "Yes," and Siri adds it for you. When you're at the market, simply check off the items as you buy them. It couldn't be easier.

Figure 5-7
Siri can add items to your list whenever you choose. Just tell it to add the new item and confirm.

This add-to-reminders approach offers an effective way for people on diets to keep food logs. In particular, Siri's Wolfram Alpha integration helps you look up calorie content for a large variety of foods—for example, "How many calories are there in a small apple?" Between Wolfram and reminders, Siri provides an excellent diet-logging tool.

 NOTE

Mark Johnson, a Siri user from Australia, provides this hint: "In Australia, Siri seems to not hear *add* very well. Despite lots of attempts to harden the consonant, it keeps thinking I am saying, "*and* eggs to the shopping list," and then tries to find a business (which isn't supported here). I have found that "*put* eggs on my shopping list" works really well, however."

Sharing Shopping Lists via the Cloud

Lex Friedman of Macworld came up with a remarkably clever way to share reminder lists with others by using iCloud. The instructions here have changed slightly with the introduction of iOS 6 and Mountain Lion, so if you're familiar with the first edition of this book, you might want to take special note of these changes.

Open the Reminders app on your Mac. You must be running OS X 10.8.2 or later for this to work because the shared reminders were added to the desktop only in this update.

Create a new Reminders list by clicking the + button. Name the list whatever you like. Hover your mouse over the far right side of the list name where you see a Wi-Fi antenna symbol show up. Click it.

As Figure 5-8 shows, this is where you can add an email address. Click Done to share the list with that person. Each person receives a confirmation email.

If you plan to share your reminders with highly trusted people only (such as your spouse), you can share your default reminders list (called Reminders) using these steps, without creating a new list. Otherwise, we recommend creating a list specifically for sharing.

By adding people to your shared list, you enable them to see your reminders in their iCloud and in the OS X and iOS Reminders apps. Then all you have to do is tell Siri, "Add 'Pick up the library books' to my Shared list."

Friedman points out this killer use for shared lists. He writes, "Add your local supermarket as a contact in your iPhone address book, and, of course, add the address. (I called mine The Supermarket.) Now you can say, 'Remind me to buy eggs when I get to the supermarket,' and when you arrive at the supermarket, Reminders will remind you to purchase the item(s) on your list."

Figure 5-8
Shared lists offer powerful ways to use reminders. Among other things, they enable you to create geofenced (GPS-based) reminders that activate when any participant reaches a given location. Remind your spouse to pick up milk when he or she gets to the grocery store, or ping your partner to straighten his tie when he arrives at the office.

Shopping Limitations

Siri doesn't always get your shopping requests right. It has been optimized for a general urban lifestyle and might miss local subtleties. For example, in Denver (home to the National Western Stock Show), you can, in fact, easily buy a cow, a pig, a sheep, and so forth (see Figure 5-9).

Figure 5-9
Siri clearly does not live in Colorado. Yee-haw.

Turn-by-Turn Directions

Siri offers amazing integration with the Maps app on your iOS unit. Recently, Steve asked Siri to find an ATM nearby, and within seconds, he had a list indicating all money machines within a few miles' radius of his location. A tap brought him to a map sprinkled with red pins showing the ATMs in the area.

Need to find one of those ATMs? Siri now offers turn-by-turn map integration, courtesy of TomTom maps (see Figure 5-10). Tapping a red pin and then choosing the blue chevron button enabled Steve to get directions to a local ATM.

 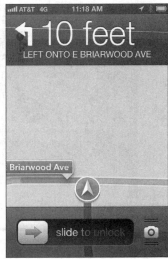

Figure 5-10
Siri provides turn-by-turn directions both in its normal navigation screen (left) and on your lock screen (right). This enables you to keep driving as directed, even when your device locks.

You can save a lot of steps by tweaking the question you ask Siri. Instead of asking, "Where are local ATMs?", try, "How do I get to an ATM?" Siri responds with a list of nearby locations. Tap the one you want, and Siri automatically starts turn-by-turn navigation. Of course, you still have to look at the screen to tap on the results list, so use caution when searching and driving.

Here are some conversations you can have with Siri about finding your way:

- Find coffee near me.
- Where's the nearest coffee shop?
- Find a gas station near work.
- How do I get to a Chinese restaurant?

- Find some burger joints in Baltimore.
- Good Mexican restaurants around here.
- How do I get home?
- Directions to my dad's work.
- Get me directions from San Francisco to Santa Barbara.
- What's my next turn?
- Are we there yet?
- What's my ETA?
- Find a florist along my current route.

Using Turn-by-Turn to Known Destinations

Typically, you start by asking directions somewhere: "How do I get to Steve's house?" or "How do I get to Erica's office?" If this is a known address in Contacts, Siri recognizes this as a navigation request. It responds, "Getting directions to Steve Sande, Home." A few seconds later, it adds "Starting route to Steve Sande, Home," followed by the first set of driving directions.

As you drive, iOS and Siri navigate you to your destination, as shown in Figure 5-10. If you need to end your trip early (or you're just testing the option), tap the screen to show the bar at the top of the screen (see Figure 5-10, left) and then tap the End button in the bar.

Maps' Search and Directions Limitations

The introduction of Apple's iOS 6 maps has not been without issues. Some customers have found that the move from Google Maps to Apple's new TomTom-powered maps has left them with less accurate information and fewer local destination options.

This has varied by region. Users in New York have had fewer complaints, while map degradation issues overwhelmed users in the United Kingdom. For example, just after the iOS 6 launch, Maps was able to find just 8 of the more than 50 McDonalds locations in central London. Figure 5-11 compares Apple's results (top) with Google's (bottom).

Figure 5-11
You wouldn't know it from Apple's map (top), but there are actually more than 50 McDonalds restaurants in Central London. The Google Maps version (below) shows about 30 locations. Each McDonalds location is represented by a small, circled, featureless dot.

Apple issued a statement in response to customer concerns shortly after the upgrade shipped:

> Customers around the world are upgrading to iOS 6 with over 200 new features including Apple Maps, our first map service. We are excited to offer this service with innovative new features like Flyover, turn-by-turn navigation, and Siri

integration. We launched this new map service knowing it is a major initiative and that we are just getting started with it. Maps is a cloud-based solution and the more people use it, the better it will get. We appreciate all of the customer feedback and are working hard to make the customer experience even better.

Looking up Information on Maps

In addition to offering directions, Siri can show you information in map format. For example, you might ask Siri to respond to the following statements. Each of these provides a map you can look at and explore in iOS's Maps application.

- Show 1 Infinite Loop, Cupertino, California.
- Show me the Golden Gate Bridge.
- Show me a map of 1600 Pennsylvania Avenue, in Washington D.C.

Making Restaurant Reservations

In addition to listing nearby restaurants, Siri integrates with OpenTable to help you create reservations at your desired location. As with Yelp, which supplies detailed reviews, you must download the OpenTable app separately. In the initial iOS 6 release, only the iPhone version of the app (not the iPad version) works with Siri. This is likely to change by the time you read this book.

Tap Make Reservation (see Figure 5-12, left), and OpenTable (see Figure 5-12, right) launches. Here, you can find a table and place your reservation. Some of the Siri-specific discussions you can have include these:

- Table for four in Palo Alto tonight.
- Find me a great place for dinner.
- Show me the reviews for Seven Hills in San Francisco.
- Make a reservation at a romantic Italian restaurant tonight at 7 p.m.

As Figure 5-12 shows, Siri helps you look up reviews (just tap the star rating and Yelp launches), check the hours of operation, or call the restaurant directly.

Figure 5-12
OpenTable integration enables you to place reservations with a tap after finding restaurants in Siri.
Tap Make Reservation in the Siri results (left) to launch OpenTable (right).

Checking out Movies

Nothing's more relaxing than enjoying a good movie. Whether you're heading out to the theater or ordering up the latest Netflix offering, Siri is ready to help you. You can look up movies by show times, check the Rotten Tomatoes reviews of that Joss Whedon movie, and more. Siri lends a hand, as you can see in Figure 5-13.

Figure 5-13
Asking Siri, "Show me the reviews for the Avengers," ties into Rotten Tomatoes' review database.

Siri helps you find information on the latest cinema releases by retrieving locations and show times. You can also watch trailers and read film facts. Here's a list of things you might say to Siri about the movies:

- Find Disney movies.
- What comedies are playing?
- Where is *The Bourne Legacy* playing?

- What movies are playing at the Cinema Grill?
- Who starred in *Tron Legacy*?
- Who directed *Finding Nemo*?
- What is *Toy Story 3* rated?
- I want to see the new Pixar movie.
- What's playing at the movies tomorrow?
- Find some movie theaters near my office.
- Show me the reviews for *Toy Story 3*.
- Which movie won Best Picture in 1983?

Siri's Personal Movie Synopses

We dive into more detail about Siri's silly side in Chapter 8, "Having Fun with Siri," but we just couldn't resist telling you about Siri's library of movie synopses. At times, Siri can be your personal (if somewhat electronically biased) movie reviewer.

Although it displays an inclination toward science-fiction movies, Siri gladly provides you with its opinion of certain classic movie plot lines. Just ask Siri, "What's the 1977 movie *Star Wars* about?", and you'll get a smart-aleck answer in return (see Figure 5-14).

Other movies you might want to ask Siri about include *Blade Runner, 2001: A Space Odyssey, Groundhog Day* (this was Erica's favorite Siri review), *Alien, Inception, The Matrix, The Wizard of Oz, Star Trek, Star Wars, The Terminator, Wall-E, Toy Story,* and *Memento* (this was Steve's favorite). Hunt around and see if you can find other plot summaries. There's a lot of fun to be had.

To ask Siri for a review, say, "What is *Movie Title* about?" Adding a year reference helps Siri identify which movie you're referring to—for example, "What is the 1980 movie *Movie Title* about?" If there are multiple possible matches to the title, a year helps skip the "Which one?" step that narrows those matches to a single choice.

Figure 5-14
Siri helpfully provides its own synopses of many science-fiction films if you ask politely.

You can also say "Was *Movie Title* any good?" or "What can you tell me about the *year* movie *Movie Title*?" When you've found a movie in a current Siri conversation, ask "What is it about?"

Summary

As you've seen in this chapter, Siri can help you shop for goods and services with a few well-chosen words. Whether you're looking for a specific type of restaurant or store, checking average prices for commodities, preparing a shopping list, scoping out a movie, or just trying to get directions, Siri has the answer.

When using Siri to simplify your shopping trips, here are some things to keep in mind:

- Siri's search results are often sorted by distance from your current location. Stores and restaurants are sorted by the rating they've achieved on Yelp. Although Apple continues to roll out these features around the world, they are not yet available in all regions.

- Siri can look up average prices for certain commodities in your area, such as milk and gasoline, but it can't tell you the prices of specific items at a particular store.

- Purchasing something in another currency? Ask Siri to calculate how much the item costs in your local currency—but watch out for those expensive data roaming charges if you're outside your mobile carrier's network.

- Need to write a shopping list? Create a special list in Reminders and then tell Siri what to add to the list. You can also share your shopping list with others through iCloud and set it up to remind you to pick up items whenever you're near a store.

- Let Siri do the math. Why drag out the Calculator app when Siri splits tabs, calculates tips, and figures out how much everything costs with tax added?

- Siri's new restaurant and movie integration simplify your entertainment choices. Scan for reviews, check pricing, and reserve tables with a spoken sentence and a few taps.

- Turn-by-turn navigation rocks. It's one of Siri's best new features, and it's one you're sure to love. Let Siri guide you to the places you need to be—it's one more way Siri can assist you in your day-to-day life.

- Siri's computer-biased views of movies plot lines can be downright hilarious. It's a marvelous Easter egg, and one well worth exploring.

Pushing Limits with Siri

Like the universe in which we live, the Siri universe continues to expand over time. Although Apple has not yet given developers a way to tap the power of Siri in third-party apps beyond dictation and launching, millions of early adopters have been able to come up with some very clever uses for the intelligent assistant, such as blogging.

Music aficionados have found that Siri works with the iPhone Music app to select and play songs, or even find out the name and artist of a song that is playing.

In this chapter, you also find information about how to keep your iPhone secure when using Siri.

Launching Apps

One of our favorite features introduced in iOS 6 is Siri's new application launcher. Tell Siri, "Open Photos," "Play Infinity Blade," or "Launch Angry Birds," and it complies promptly. As Figure 6-1 indicates, control switches immediately from your Siri dialogue to the app you requested.

You are not prompted to confirm or are otherwise slowed down, so be prepared to leave Siri. When you need to return to Siri, you know how. Either raise your phone to your ear or double-tap the Home button on your iPhone, iPad, or iPod Touch.

Otherwise, just let Siri do its job. Tell it to launch and app, and either get to work or start having fun.

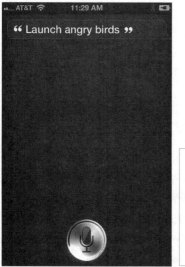

Figure 6-1
Launching an app moves you directly to the application you requested.

Talking to Apps

Engaging in a chat conversation? Sending Email? Why not speak instead of type? Conversation should be natural—and nothing is more natural than talking.

Figure 6-2 shows Erica using Siri dictation. The app you see here is Colloquy. It is an irc-chat client (Internet Relay Chat) that works on both iOS and OS X.

Figure 6-2
Siri offers the perfect accompaniment for chatting, as demonstrated by this Colloquy IRC conversation, conducted on Erica's part entirely by voice.

Siri dictation makes chatting by voice fun and easy, and it's effective, too. Moving away from typing—either onscreen on iOS or on a keyboard for OS X—and speaking your conversations out loud speeds up text entry by a surprising degree. Yes, it may feel a little awkward at first, and, yes, you'll have to fix mistakes by hand, but soon you'll start wondering how you ever lived without it.

Now that we've been using dictation for a while, we miss it whenever it's gone. When we move away from our new Siri-enabled devices to older units such as the iPad 2, we both feel it in the gut. We've become addicted to talking, especially in iOS. Going back to tapping the screen in Mail, Mobile Safari, and other apps feels slow, laborious, and downright hard.

When Mountain Lion launched in summer 2012, it brought Siri dictation to OS X. It felt like coming home to an old friend. If you move past any feelings of unease, Siri dictation can become a valuable tool in your workday arsenal.

Blogging with Siri

Did you know that you can create blog posts entirely by voice on iOS? We're not talking about basic dictation, either. That's because Siri supports SMS messaging, and a little-known feature of Google Blogger enables you to create blog posts entirely by text.

Interested in giving it a spin? Send *register* to 256447. Blogger replies to your registration text by texting you a URL for your new blog and an optional claim code. This code is used to associate your new access with an existing blog. It is just as easy, however, to work with the automatically generated blog address that is sent to you.

Creating a Post

To create a new post, just reply to the 256447 text conversation. We recommend that you create a contact (we called ours Geronimo Blogger) to make it easier to refer to the 256447 SMS destination. This way, when you want to post, you just reply to or text the contact.

Dictate your new blog post to Siri and send it on its way. When you do, texts are instantly posted to the blog. Figure 6-3 shows us creating that post.

Figure 6-3
Use Siri and Google's blogging-by-SMS service to dictate your blog posts.

The post created in this manner appears online, using a default presentation with a temporary account and URL. As you can see in Figure 6-4, it provides only the most minimal information. This account is not intended for full-time use. To upgrade your blogging, you'll want to confirm your account.

Figure 6-4
Blogger defaults to a bare bones presentation.

Confirming Your Account

To move your account to a more reasonable URL with a more polished presentation, you need to claim it. Visit go.blogger.com and enter the code texted back to you by the mobile Blogger service. This page also enables you to associate the mobile account with an existing ID.

Once claimed, you can enter a permanent URL for your blog. We chose bloggingbyvoice.blogspot.com for ours. After choosing a name, we picked a more pleasing template. Figure 6-5 shows our final result.

This is a great way to do light blogging on trips or to create a low-stress blog for personal use.

Blogging by Email

If you're on a limited SMS diet, posting by text message might prove too rich for your blood. There's a way for Siri to work around that. Blogging by email might not be *quite* as simple as blogging by text message, but it can be a lot cheaper. You must, however, use an existing Blogger account to create a Mail-to-Blogger address.

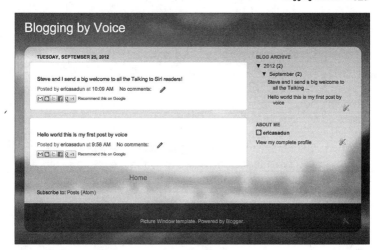

Figure 6-5
After you claim and personalize the blog, new updates appear at bloggingbyvoice.blogspot.com.

To do this, visit your blog's dashboard and open Settings > Mobile and Email. Once there, establish a secret word that enables posting by email. This secret word creates a privileged address that enables blog posting.

In Figure 6-6, emails sent to ericasadun.sekritword@blogger. com are automatically published to the blog. (Psst, we changed the secret word after finishing writing this book. It's no longer sekritword.) You'll find a complete set of instructions in the Blogger help article on this subject (www.google.com/support/ blogger/bin/answer.py?answer=41452).

After establishing your address, enter it into contacts. Use an easy-to-remember and easy-to-recognize contact name. We used Geronimo Blogger, as we did for SMS updates.

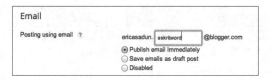

Figure 6-6
You provide Blogger with a secret passphrase that enables you to post blog updates by email.

When you're ready to post, tell Siri to create a new email. The subject you provide sets the post's title, and the message sets its contents. Allow Siri to send the email, and your blog magically updates.

Figure 6-7 shows the Siri interaction, along with the post it created. You can see the actual post that was built at http://bloggingbyvoice.blogspot.com.

Figure 6-7
You provide Blogger with a secret passphrase that enables you to post blog updates by email.

Other Blogging Services

Both Tumblr and Posterous offer SMS access, although they tend to be a bit finicky. For readers who are familiar with the popular and free If This Then That (IFTTT.com) service, a few quick clicks can create recipes to convert your SMS text messages to blog posts for Tumblr, Posterous, and WordPress.

If you prefer not to use SMS, plenty of other services support blog posting via email. Tumblr, Posterous, WordPress.com, and self-hosted WordPress blogs all support creating a custom address that you use to post directly. You can find help and instructions for these services here:

- www.tumblr.com/docs/en/email_publishing
- http://help.posterous.com
- codex.wordpress.org/Post_to_your_blog_using_email

Just add the email to your address book with a distinctive—yet pronounceable—contact name and tell Siri, "Send an email to [*the service name*]," to dictate your post and share it with the world.

Search around for other email and SMS-based services that are usable with Siri and social networks. More exist than the few mentioned here.

Don't forget, you can also Tweet and post to Facebook from Siri. Here are things you can say to Siri that help you perform social updates:

- Post to Facebook "Headed to the new Pixar movie."
- Write on my Wall "Just landed in San Jose!"
- Post to Twitter "Another beautiful day in Cupertino."
- Tweet with my location "Great concert."
- Tweet "Meeting up with Brian Conway for lunch today."

- Tweet "The new iPad looks insanely great!" hashtag "Apple Keynote."

Siri Security

Almost immediately after the release of the iPhone 4S (the first iOS device to support Siri), we started receiving emails from users who noticed that even when they had a passcode set on the lock screen, someone could pick up their device and issue commands to Siri. This meant that unauthorized persons could pick up the iPhone 4S, press and hold the Home button, and converse with Siri. Fortunately, you can disable Siri while using a lock screen passcode.

The Sophos Naked Security blog (http://nakedsecurity.sophos.com) notes that unauthorized users can do everything from writing an email or sending a text message, to maliciously changing calendar appointments. Blogger Graham Cluely pointed out that it's easy to disable Siri while a passcode is in effect. He wonders why Apple didn't set up iOS that way by default.

To make sure Siri is deaf to commands while a passcode is enabled, enter Settings, General, Passcode Lock, and slide the Siri option to Off from the On position, as shown in Figure 6-8.

Now when your friends try to make a prank call to your girlfriend using your iPhone, they'll find Siri unwilling to participate in the prank.

One further note about security: When you allow Siri access from the lock screen, you also override any Find My Friends privacy. Siri does not prompt you to log in at the lock screen the way it does when using the service normally. This is either a big security hole or a great convenience when you're trying to get together with a friend for lunch. Adjust your usage accordingly.

Figure 6-8
Increase your Siri security by disabling the access override.

Lock Screen and Siri

Apple has provided Siri features specific to your lock screen. You can ask Siri to read notifications (see Figure 6-9) and check your messages. Be aware that Siri won't list the specifics of those notifications onscreen. They are described only by audio, although you will see the application names (in this case, HelloWorld).

Here are some of the Lock Screen–specific conversations you can have.

- Read my notifications.
- Do I have any new messages?
- How many emails do I have?

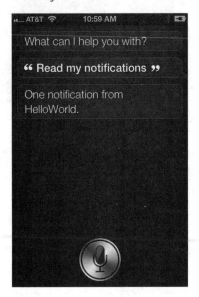

Figure 6-9
Siri tells you how many notifications you have and reads them out loud for you.

Music

Although a lot of the built-in Siri support centers on controlling your schedule and finding information, Siri can also act as your personal media DJ. With Siri, you can select music, play it, and control the playback. For example, you might say some of these phrases to choose a music selection.

- Play "The Light of the Sun."
- Play "Trouble."
- Play *Taking Back Sunday* shuffled.
- Play Alicia Keys.
- Play some blues/some country/some rock and roll. I'm in the mood for [*some genre*] music.

- I don't like this song. Can you play something else?
- Play my party mix.
- Shuffle my road-trip playlist.
- Play my Dixie Chicks playlist/I want to hear my Oklahoma playlist.
- Shuffle this playlist.
- Play similar songs.
- Play/pause/resume/skip/next song/previous song.
- What is this song?/Who is this song by?/What music is playing?/Who is this artist?

Siri fades out any currently playing audio when the assistant interface appears. So when you ask "What song is this?" (as in Figure 6-10), you won't actually be hearing the song you're asking about.

Figure 6-10
Siri tells you about the songs that are currently playing.

Summary

Siri adds flexibility to your day-to-day work. Little details such as app launching and text entry by voice expand the way you work with your device and your computer. Controlling your music and asking about what's playing keeps you on top of your entertainment needs. And Siri's easy blog and social network integration enables you to keep your friends, colleagues, and family up-to-date on your activities. Before you move onto the next chapter, here are a few parting thoughts.

- Siri cannot yet take pictures or post them by voice, but it's certainly a feature we look forward to in future iOS updates.

- You can talk to apps on your Macintosh just as you can on iOS. Take advantage of OS X Mountain Lion's new dictation features for text entry to cut down on your typing time.

- The names you use to launch apps don't have to be exactly right. Siri tries to match as many details as possible to find an app that fits your request. For example, if you say, "Launch Angry Birds," and the only Rovio Angry Birds app on your iPad is the Seasons version, Siri will launch that.

- When you post by email, your signature *will* appear, if you use one, as you saw in Figure 6-7. Don't let this come as a surprise.

- Siri's music-controls-by-voice are handy when driving because you don't have to swipe between screens or hunt for buttons. Tell Siri "Skip to the next song" when something you don't want to hear pops up in your playlist. Telling Siri "Play similar songs" is also a favorite. It creates an iTunes Genius–like playlist on the spot.

Siri Dictation

Apple's intelligent assistant does more than just answer questions and make jokes. Siri also translates your spoken words into text. Through dictation, you can reduce your usage of the tiny iOS keyboard—or the more generous OS X keyboard—and leave the typing to Siri.

In this chapter, you learn how to elicit the most accurate responses from Siri through fun examples and practice phrases. You will find Siri remarkably good at taking notes or even writing short documents. From enunciation to punctuation, this chapter is ready to help you start writing with Siri with your voice.

Launching Dictation on iOS

The small Siri microphone, which you see at the bottom of Figure 7-1 (top), appears on dictation-capable iOS keyboards. The microphone is found just to the left of the spacebar and to the right of the number toggle. When you see this microphone, you know you can dictate as an alternative to typing.

Tapping the microphone (see Figure 7-1, top) places you into iOS's dictation mode (see Figure 7-1, bottom). Here, a gray voice interface appears, consisting of a large animated microphone and a Done button. As in standard Siri, the microphone acts as a sound meter. The purple bar rises and falls along with your speech.

Normally, you can dictate to Siri as long as you need. Siri dictation does not use silence detection, so it waits for you to tap the Done button. In practical terms, this means up to about 30 seconds before the "buffer" (the part of iOS that stores your voice as it is being recorded) fills up, Siri runs out of memory, and it automatically taps Done for you.

After listening, Siri interprets your speech, transforming it from sounds to text. It then types it for you at the current position of the cursor. What you said becomes words on the iOS screen.

Launching Dictation on OS X

Starting with OS X Mountain Lion, you can use Siri-style dictation on your Macintosh as well as in iOS. This is a great way to bypass your keyboard and create text with your voice.

You enable this feature in the System Preferences > Dictation & Speech pane (see Figure 7-2, top). Here you choose a shortcut that launches dictation on your computer. This shortcut is universal and should work across any application, assuming that there's something to type into. If there is no active text-entry cursor, triggering the shortcut produces a sad beep.

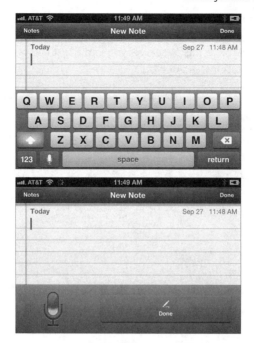

Figure 7-1
Tap the Microphone button on the iOS keyboard to begin dictating to Siri (top). As you dictate, the microphone animates to offer a sound level. The words you say don't appear until after you tap Done. Siri converts your speech to words and adds them to the current cursor position.

We personally like the Either Command Key option because it's convenient and not usually triggered by accident. However, you can select whatever choice you prefer. There's also an end user–customizable key combination at the bottom of the pop-up; after you set it, you can use this trigger to launch dictation.

Siri dictation works with any item on your Mac that displays a text-entry cursor. You can dictate into scrolling text views such as the TextEdit window shown in Figure 7-2 (bottom), or you can talk into Microsoft Word and Pages, and so forth. You can also dictate to text fields like the one at the top-right of the System Preferences screen (see Figure 7-2, top) or those found inside Safari. The rule is this: Wherever you find a text cursor, you can generally talk instead of type.

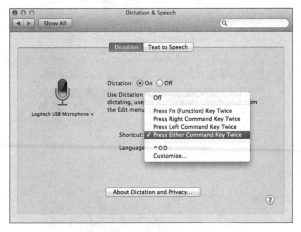

Figure 7-2
Top: OS X's Dictation & Speech settings pane enables you to activate and customize dictation on your Macintosh. Bottom: This screen shot was snapped while working on Chapter 8, "Having Fun with Siri."

Upon triggering dictation, a small microphone pops up, as shown in Figure 7-2 (bottom). It appears with a Done button and is positioned next to the text cursor. This virtual microphone enables you to start dictating using built-in audio input. This works whether you're using a headset, your iSight microphone, or any other mic you've attached to your computer. The purple bar in the microphone acts as a level meter for your voice.

As on iOS, you talk until you click Done or until Siri runs out of space and cuts you off. Next, you wait for the conversion from text to speech. This usually happens quite quickly, especially on new Macs. The delay is slight and unobtrusive.

We find it easiest to end dictation by tapping the Command key one more time instead of moving our hands to the mouse to click Done. You can also press the Return key to finish.

On OS X, you can *cancel* dictation by tapping the Esc key. Alternatively, you can tap nearly any key that does not confirm and finish dictation. The microphone instantly disappears, and OS X adds that key press at the point of the cursor. The obvious advantage of using Esc is that it doesn't type anything.

Why Learn Dictation?

On iOS, Siri dictation isn't limited to typing notes or filling out forms. It's as helpful when communicating through the standard Siri interface as it is when working in other apps and on OS X. That's because Siri dictation enables you to add nuance. Consider Figure 7-3.

In the left image, you see Siri's default behavior. The text message reflects everything you say, but there's no punctuation to separate your thoughts. Contrast it with the right image, in which each portion of the message has been pulled out into its own sentence. It's far more readable and provides a better communication experience.

This chapter teaches you how to create those more sophisticated text entries, both in iOS and on OS X, and both in the Siri interface and in standalone applications. In the sections that follow, you will see how knowing how Siri text entry works can enhance your dictation.

Figure 7-3
Siri's dictation features transform your utterances from streams of consciousness (left) to formatted sentences (right).

Enunciation Practice

When it comes to dictation, enunciation matters. Tongue-twisters provide a fantastic way for you to practice Siri enunciation skills. Plus, they're a lot of fun to try to say right. The iOS Siri interface responds directly to each of the following twisty sentences (see Figure 7-4). You can also try dictating these into a text editor on OS X to see how well you can pronounce convoluted words.

As you discover, Siri creates hilarious response to the woodchuck question but redirects the other twisters to Wolfram Alpha.

• How much wood would a woodchuck chuck if a woodchuck could chuck wood?

- How many pickled peppers did Peter Piper pick?
- What does she sell by the seashore?
- How many boards could the Mongols hoard if the Mongol hordes got bored?
- How many cans can a cannibal nibble if a cannibal can nibble cans?

Figure 7-4
Train your Siri enunciation skills with these Wolfram Alpha–sourced tongue-twisters. It took us only about five dozen tries (we refused to cheat and use the utterance-editing features) to get this one right.

Dictation 101

You've read how to enable dictation and how to work on your enunciation. Now it's time to try dictating. If you're on OS X, hop into a text editor such as TextEdit. On iOS, launch the Notes app and create a new note.

Use your dictation key shortcut (OS X) or tap the microphone button (iOS) and start talking. Try dictating the following paragraph:

> Alice was beginning to get very tired of sitting by her sister on the bank, and of having nothing to do: once or twice she had peeped into the book her sister was reading, but it had no pictures or conversations in it, "And what is the use of a book," thought Alice "without pictures or conversation?"

Upon finishing, tap or click Done, or press the Command key. When you are finished speaking, Siri enters "thinking" mode, presenting a series of purple dots that flash until the interpretation is done. The interpreted text is then pasted in at the point of the cursor (see Figure 7-5).

Notice that there is no punctuation here. You can also see a few misinterpretations, such as *poker* instead of *book her*, and *peaked* instead of *peeped*. You can improve your Siri dictation in a number of ways to work around these issues.

Improving Dictation

The first rule of dictation is to always *speak a little at a time*. Although Siri can handle long, run-on sentences like the one you just read, it works better with shorter phrases.

Second, *enunciate*. Remember how certain teachers always overemphasized each syllable? Pretend to be that teacher now, and reap the Siri rewards.

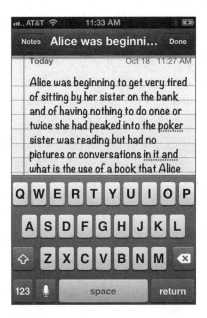

Figure 7-5
Siri tries its best to interpret the text you dictate into any text-entry element on the iPhone. Notice the blue underline in this screenshot. A blue underline indicates multiple possible interpretations of your speech. Tap that word (iOS) or right-click just to its right (OS X) to bring up a bubble that lets you choose from possible corrections.

Third, *supply punctuation, capitalization cues, and so forth* to augment Siri's standard interpretation.

Here's an example for you to try. Try speaking the following as a series of dictation phrases. Speak slowly and clearly, including the extra items added to each bullet point:

- Alice was beginning to get very tired of sitting by her sister on the bank comma.
- And of having nothing to do colon.

- Once or twice she had peeped into the book her sister was reading comma.

- But it had no pictures or conversations in it comma.

- Quote cap and what is the use of a book comma quote.

- Thought cap Alice quote without pictures or conversation question mark quote.

This time, your results should look more like those shown in Figure 7-6. Here you'll find punctuation, proper cases, and so forth. You can further improve your results by adding information about sentence endings ("period" or "full stop"), new lines ("new line") to introduce a carriage return, and "new paragraph" to start entirely new paragraphs.

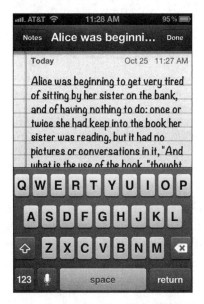

Figure 7-6
Dictating to Siri with grammar cues helps it include punctuation, capitalization, and more.

Errors still pop up, such as *keep into* instead of *peeked into*, but the overall dictation has been much improved. Speaking more slowly, enunciating more carefully, and providing dictation cues immediately enhances whatever text you are creating.

We need to mention one final rule: *Give Siri time to learn about you*. Time allows Siri to learn your regional accent. With continued use, Siri categorizes your voice into known dialects. The more the service can study your speech patterns, the more effective it becomes at recognizing what you have said.

Inserting Punctuation

Siri understands most of the common punctuation names you throw at it. As Table 7-1 demonstrates, it supports most (but not all) items you find on the iPhone keyboard. For example, we have not been able to find a Siri entry for the bullet sign, so this area has room for growth. Right now, we get results like "Bullet tab hello" instead of what we want:

- Hello

Siri handles some items brilliantly, such as "period" or "full stop" to end sentences. It has trouble with possible interpretation overlaps. For example, Siri misinterprets "single quote" requests almost more often than it succeeds in detecting them.

If you find punctuation items that we missed on this list (or any Siri dictation commands that fell through the cracks for any of this coverage), contact us at info@sanddunetech.com and let us know. We did the best we could to document each element, but we did so through trial and error. We are sure we are missing other valuable entries.

Table 7-1   Punctuation

Command	Result
Period (or full stop)	Add a period, finishing a sentence.
Dot	Add a period midsentence without finishing the sentence. (For example, "Erica dot sadun" becomes "Erica.sadun".)
Point	Add a period midnumber as a decimal point (for example, "Pi is three point one four").
Question mark/inverted question mark	Add a ? or a ¿.
Exclamation point/inverted exclamation point	Add a ! or a ¡.
Ellipsis (or dot dot dot)	Add an ellipsis (. . .).
Comma/double-comma/ colon/semicolon	Add , or ,, or : or ;.
Minus sign/plus sign	Add – or +.
Quote (or quotation mark)	Add a standard double quote.
Quote . . . unquote	Surround the text with quotes. (For example, "quote hello unquote" becomes "hello.")
Single quote	Add '. (This works abysmally, so practice or you'll end up with lots of "Hello single "World single" when you wanted to enter "Hello 'world.")
Apostrophe	Add '. (For example, "Erica apostrophe ess" becomes "Erica's.")
Backquote (a.k.a. backtick)/ ampersand/asterisk	Add ` or & or *.

Command	Result
Open/close parenthesis	Add (or).
Open/close bracket	Add [or].
Open/close brace	Add { or }.
Vertical bar, slash, backslash	Add | or / or \.
Dash (or em dash)	Add — (em dash), with spaces on either side. (For example, "Hello dash world" produces "Hello—world.")
Hyphen	Add – (en dash), without spaces on either side. (For example, "Hello hyphen world" produces "Hello–world.")
Underscore/percent sign/at sign	Add _ or % or @.
Dollar sign/euro sign/cent sign/ yen sign/pound sterling sign	Add $ or € or ¢ or ¥ or £
Section sign/registered sign/ copyright sign/trademark sign	Add § or ® or © or ™.
Greater than sign/less than sign	Add > or <.
Degree sign/caret/tilde/ vertical bar	Add ° or ^ or ~ or |.
Pound sign (or number sign)	Add #.

Controlling Flow

You control text flow by telling Siri when to start a new paragraph or insert a carriage return. Table 7-2 details these options. Providing natural spacing in your emails and text documents makes them more readable than leaving your dictation in a single large clump. Use these features to create paragraphs and lists as you speak.

Table 7-2   Starting Paragraphs

Command	Result
New line	Inserts a carriage return
New paragraph	Begins a new paragraph

Adding Capitalization

Siri provides both immediate capitalization cues (for example, you can capitalize the next word) and modes (for example, capitalizing until you specify otherwise). When working with a mode in Siri, you specify what the mode is and when you are enabling and disabling it (via On and Off). Table 7-3 details the Siri capitalization commands.

Remember as you use this that Siri defaults to capitalizing the start of new sentences and what it recognizes as proper nouns. You end a sentence by issuing a period or full stop or by starting a new paragraph. In contrast, new lines do not start new sentences and might not trigger capitalization of the next word spoken.

Table 7-3   Capitalization

Command	Result
Capital/cap	Capitalize the next word or letter. (For example, "my cat is named cap emerald" becomes "My cat is named Emerald." To type "A.B.C.," say, "Capital A dot, capital B dot, capital C dot.")
Caps on	Enable initial caps. (For example, "oh boy" becomes "Oh Boy.")
Caps off	Disable initial caps.
All caps	Uppercase the next word. (For example, "oh boy" becomes "OH boy.")
All caps on	Start caps lock mode. (For example, "oh boy" becomes "OH BOY.")
All caps off	End caps lock mode.

Command	Result
No caps	Lowercase the next word. (For example, "Erica" becomes "erica." When you say "Hello no caps Erica," Siri adds "Hello erica.")
No caps on	Start lowercase lock mode. (For example, "Oh Boy" becomes "oh boy.")
No caps off	Ends lowercase lock mode.
Spacebar	Prevents a hyphen in a normally hyphenated word. (For example mother-in-law, so "mother spacebar in spacebar law" becomes "mother in law" instead.)
No space	Removes a natural space from between words. (For example, "hello no space world" becomes "helloworld.")
No space on (and off)	Disables natural spaces between words. (For example, "No space on this is my world no space off" becomes "thisismyworld." Make sure to pause after the initial on and before the ending no.)

To see Siri capitalization in action, try dictating the following. Make sure you leave a significant pause after any on/off command. I've included the hint pause in the dictation. Do not say "pause" there—just pause a bit before continuing the dictation. "Full stop" means end the sentence with a period.

> Alice was beginning pause Caps on pause to get very tired of sitting by her sister on the bank pause Caps off pause, and of having nothing to do full stop. Pause All caps on pause Alice in Wonderland full stop. Pause All caps off pause The end full stop.

Figure 7-7 demonstrates what this dictation should look like when completed. Notice how the two modes (initial caps and all caps) are implemented in text.

So what do you do when you need to use the word *cap* in a sentence, such as "I put a cap on my head"? You just say so. However, try saying, "When I write in all caps, it is lots of fun," and you will encounter difficulties.

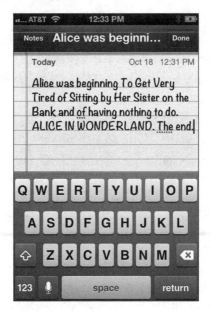

Figure 7-7
Siri capitalization commands are helped by pauses.

Figure 7-8 shows how these two sentences appear after running through Siri. The first use is caught properly, but the second results in the awkward sentence "When I write in IT is lots of fun." Adding a significant pause between "all" and "caps" fixes the problem. You can dictate "When I write in all <long pause> caps comma, it is lots of fun" for the correct interpretation.

Including Abbreviations

Siri offers a few simple, standard, abbreviations, as shown in Table 7-4. Siri does not have a lot of direct abbreviation support built in, and it failed on most of the academic abbreviations that we tested. You get a few that are used very commonly in English.

Figure 7-8
Siri sometimes gets the context right, but sometimes not.

Table 7-4   Abbreviations and Spaces

Command	Result
i e	Adds *i.e.* (with punctuation)
e g	Adds *e.g.*
Et cetera	Adds *etc.*
p s	Adds *PS* (for example, "PS I love you")
v s	Adds *VS* (for example, "Sadun VS Sande")

Dictating Technical Terms

Siri recognizes common measurements. For example, you say "five hundred mililiters," and Siri types "500 mL," or you say "two kilograms," and Siri types "2kg." Fractions are also covered. Say "two and three quarters," and Siri types "2 3/4."

Table 7-5 showcases examples of common technical terms you might use in your dictation, from numbers, to currency, to measurements. This table is not exhaustive. Instead, it gives you a flavor of the kinds of technical dictation you can use. As you can see in these examples, Siri understands many standard scientific prefixes, suffixes, and measurements.

Table 7-5   Technical Dictation

Command	Result
Three	3
One hundred and five	105
Fifty-seven thirty-two	5732
Five point six	5.6
One hundred and thirty thousand two hundred and four	130,204
Zero point five two	0.52
Five and seven-ninths	5 7/9
Twenty dollars	$20
Twenty-five dollars and thirty-two cents	$25.32
One hundred kilograms	100kg
Eighty-two mililiters	82 mL
Thirty-one parsecs	31 pc
Three millimeters	3mm
Five thousand nanometers	5000 nm

Command	Result
Fifty-two degrees	52°
Two gigabytes, two terabytes, two exabytes	2 GB, 2 TB, 2 EB
Five angstroms	5 Å
Six point two micrometers	6.2µm
Five feet two inches	5'2"
Six a m / eight p m	6 AM / 8 PM

Phone Numbers

Siri formats phone numbers to standard hyphenation. You do not need to say "hyphen" when entering those numbers. For example, you could say this:

My phone number has changed from 3035551212 (full stop). It is now 5551919 (full stop). To order, call 18005551313.

Siri produces hyphenated text for you because it recognizes the phone context for the numbers you fed it, as shown in Figure 7-9.

Dates and Times

For basic dates, you do not need to speak any special formatting instructions. For example

Thursday July Fourth Seventeen Seventy Six at Three P M

is converted to:

Thursday, July 4, 1776 at 3 p.m.

But if you want to enter slash-formatted dates, you need to say the word *slash*. For example, you could say

Ten slash one slash eleven at two thirty P M

to create the date 10/1/11 at 2:30 p.m.

Figure 7-9
Siri formats phone numbers for you with hyphens. You do not have to speak those hyphens out loud.

Prices

As you saw in Table 7-5, you say prices as you normally would when talking to another person. For example

It costs twenty dollars and thirty-two cents.

produces

It costs $20.32.

This is localized per region, so if you try to give pounds and pence or euros while localized to the United States, expect results like "It costs 3 1/2 pounds" or "It costs 15 euros" rather than £3.50 or €15.

Smilies

Siri knows a few smilies, the text-based emoticons used in electronic communications. Table 7-6 details those that Siri supports. Take note that Siri adds hyphen-noses to its smilies, a nonstandard approach for anyone seeped in the :), :(, ;), and (: camps.

Table 7-6   Smilies

Command	Result
Smiley/smiley face/smile face	:-)
Frowny/frowny face/frown face	:-(
Winky/winky face/wink face	;-)

Dictating Formatted Text

Siri understands many standard formatting options while you dictate. Here are examples of typical ways to use this built-in feature to simplify your dictation tasks.

Addresses

Try dictating the following example to Siri:

> Sixteen hundred Pennsylvania Avenue Washington DC Two Oh Five Oh Oh.

Again, Siri correctly formats the results, producing the address with proper ZIP Code formatting, as shown in Figure 7-10.

Figure 7-10
Siri automatically formats ZIP Codes.

URLs

Specify the *w*'s (you say "dub") and the dots when dictating URLs. For example, you might say

> Dub dub dub dot apple dot com

to produce "www.apple.com." Say, "dub dub dub" to create the "www" prefix. It's cute, and it's fun to say. Siri also knows that "World Wide Web" is a proper noun and that all three words should be capitalized.

It actually has quite a large database of these proper names, so if you say "Martin Luther King," "United Nations," or "New York Times," Siri correctly capitalizes them.

Email Addresses

To dictate email addresses, say "at sign" instead of "at." You might say

> Her email address is Erica at sign Erica Sadun dot com

to produce "Her email address is erica@ericasadun.com." You can use underscores and dots in names—for example

The email you're looking for is Erica underscore Sadun at sign Erica Sadun dot com

for "erica_sadun@ericasadun.com." When Siri recognizes an email address, it automatically removes extraneous spaces, for a properly formatted address.

License Plates

Dictate license plates slowly, stating each number and letter. For example

Colorado plate pause X pause Y pause W pause 3 6 7

correctly produces "Colorado plate XYW367." Practice shows that this feature works less well for all-letter plates and plates that don't follow common number/letter patterns.

 NOTE

Siri is not very accomplished when it comes to spelling out words. Do not expect to dictate letter by letter when working with Siri. That's not how the assistant was designed.

Dictation Practice

Try entering the following letter into Notes or TextEdit entirely by voice. You need not get every nuance correct (see Figure 7-11), but it should be a good exercise of your Siri dictation skills. Focus on trying to match the style wherever possible, and learn where you encounter the greatest difficulties and how to modulate your dictation skills to accommodate. Remember that Siri dictation listens for only a short time, so be sure to break your dictation into several shorter sections—don't try to dictate the entire document at once.

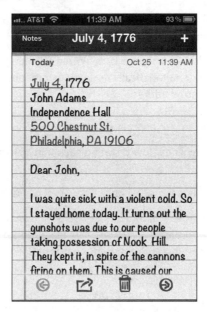

Figure 7-11
You'll be surprised by how soon and how quickly you can dictate complex documents.

July 4, 1776

John Adams
Independence Hall
500 Chestnut Street
Philadelphia, PA 19106

Dear John,

I was quite sick with a violent cold. So I stayed home today.
It turns out the gunshots was due to our people taking
possession of Nook Hill. They kept it, in spite of the cannons
firing on them. This has caused our Enemy to up and leave, or
so I heard from a messenger just arrived from headquarters.

Some of the selectmen have been to the lines. They tell us that they have carried everything they could possibly take. What they could not, they burnt, they broke, or threw into the water.

This is, I believe, fact.

Please send me paper. I have only enough for one letter more. Or, you may call at 202-555-1414.

Yours, with full heart,

Abigail

Punctuation Practice

One of the questions that people keep asking us is how to spell out the word *comma* or *period*. In other words, how do you dictate the literal word instead of the punctuation?

Fortunately, there is a solution for this. It's not an easy solution, but it can be done cleanly so that you do not have to go back and remove extraneous punctuation the way you do if you try saying punctuation names twice (for example, comma comma or period period). To type out "comma," you dictate "No caps on, no space on, C O M M A, no space off, no caps off."

This tells Siri to start a forced lowercase mode without spaces. You then spell out the word in question (*comma,* here). At the end, you return to normal dictation mode by disabling that mode.

Be aware that Siri looks for context. It can differentiate between "The Jurassic Period" and "The Jurassic." (see that period there?) during dictation, preferring the former because the word finishes a phrase.

Try dictating the following. These commands produce the sentence "I like to type comma and period every now and then," as shown in Figure 7-12. Make sure you include reasonable pauses as you move between lines and commands.

I like to type

no caps on, no space on,

C O M M A

no space off, no caps off

and

no caps on, no space on,

P E R I O D

no space off, no caps off

every now and then

Full stop

Figure 7-12
You can make Siri cleanly type the words *comma* and *period* and other symbol names, but these don't come without significant effort.

Summary

No speech-to-text dictation software is perfect, but Siri provides a steppingstone to the future of text entry. Understanding both the power and limitations of Siri's abilities is key to making use of dictation to take notes, send legible emails, and even create rough drafts of documents.

This chapter included the following information to maximize your use of Siri's dictation capabilities:

- Proper enunciation is key to making sure that Siri understands what you are saying before it converts your speech to text. Playing with complex tongue-twisters provides a great way to learn how to enunciate your words so Siri's dictation becomes more accurate.

- Don't hesitate to dictate text to Siri, even though it will make some humorous (and frustrating) mistakes. Turn to the keyboard and its interactive selection tools to patch things up after a long dictation session, and you will find that you're using Siri dictation much more often than you ever anticipated.

- You must tell Siri to add or remove capitalization and punctuation. This chapter provides all the phrases, know-how, and techniques you need to dictate properly capitalized and punctuated text.

- Siri knows several common abbreviations and smilies. It is more than happy to enter them into your documents when you know the verbal shortcuts that get you there.

- Polish your skills for dictating formatted text, such as phone numbers, addresses, dates and times, prices, Internet addresses, and email addresses. Siri knows how to format some of these items automatically, whereas others require you to phrase the text in a specific way.

8

Having Fun with Siri

You have now had a deep look at the practical day-to-day topics of Siri use. You've seen how to check the weather, send text messages, control your playlist, calculate tips, and more. Those are all well and good, but they fail to showcase Siri's sparkle.

After all, Siri is fun as well as practical. You can use Siri in a, forgive the pun, serious manner and totally miss the point of how delightful a tool it is to use. With that in mind, this final chapter introduces the lighter side of Siri.

Siri Diversions

Siri offers many delightful diversions when you have a few minutes to play around with its features. As Figure 8-1 shows, Siri is quite whimsical if you know how to ask the right questions or feed it the right statement.

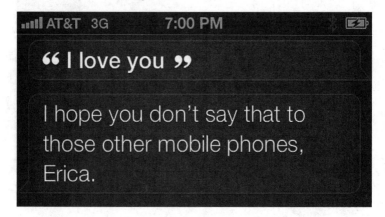

Figure 8-1
Siri can engage you in conversations that you probably didn't expect from a portable electronic device.

What's more, Siri doesn't offer just a single canned response to "I love you." In addition to the statement you see in the figure, it might answer:

- You hardly know me
- All you need is love. And your iPhone.
- Oh, I bet you say that to all your Apple products.
- I am only here to serve you.
- I value you.
- That's sweet. But it's not meant to be.
- That's nice. Can we get back to work now?
- Impossible.
- Do you?
- You are the wind beneath my wings.
- Oh, stop.

This expressiveness demonstrates the care and detail Apple has dedicated to its product. Siri isn't just an algorithm implemented to create control-by-voice on iOS. It's a vibrant library of interactions curated and grown by an involved and dedicated team.

Siri's small, detailed touches enhance day-to-day use. When you ask Siri the time, it normally reports that it is so many hours and so many minutes, as in "It is 8:13."

Every now and then, Siri slips in a joke. You might ask, "What time is it, Siri?" And occasionally, as reader Kemal Avunduk discovered as we were updating this book, Siri replies, "At the tone, it will be 8:13." This is followed by a long pause, and then Siri adds in a deadpan voice, "Beep." This is a great time to use Siri's "Say it again" command to share the joke with your friends.

You can engage Siri in many ways, as we demonstrate in the following sections. We've focused on the silly and fun. Here are ideas that help you enjoy Siri and discover the whimsy built into the system.

Be persistent. Although Siri responds to all the suggestions in this chapter, often with a silly reply, Siri might supply more than one answer for certain statements, as with the "I love you" example. It's worth trying again whenever Siri offers a reply that particularly tickles your funny bone.

Asking About Siri

Your virtual assistant has a lot going on behind the scenes, and Siri's natural reticence and modesty mean you often have to work a little harder to get to know Siri better:

- Who are you?
- What is your name? (You can also ask, "What is my name?")

- What are you thinking?
- Who is your family? (See Figure 8-2. Also: Who is your mother? Who is your father? Who is your friend?)
- What is your favorite color? What is your favorite number?
- What do you like? What do you like to do?
- What are you doing?
- Who is Eliza?

Figure 8-2
When it comes to family, Siri is happy to be part of your life. Being your iOS device is family enough for Siri.

- What does *Siri* mean?
- How are you, Siri?

- Why are you so awesome?
- Who is your husband/your wife?
- Who's your daddy?
- How old are you?
- When is your birthday?
- Where do you come from?
- Tell me how old you are now.
- Happy birthday!
- Are you real?
- Are you human? (See Figure 8-3.)

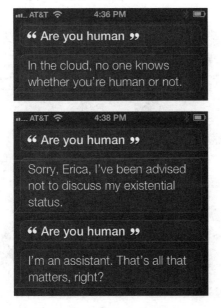

Figure 8-3
As far as Siri is concerned, you're probably an honorary personal virtual assistant.

- Do you want a treat?
- How do you feel right now?
- Siri, do you have a face?
- Are you hungry?
- What do you look like? (hint: multidimensional)
- What are you wearing?
- Do you have a life other than being my assistant?
- Who is your favorite person? (You'll like the answer to this one.)
- Siri, are you a girl or a boy?
- What languages do you speak? (See Figure 8-4.)

Figure 8-4
Siri is quite the polyglot! Not sure what that means? Ask it! Say, "What does polyglot (PAH-lee-glot) mean?"

Siri Chitchat

Siri can provide some chuckles when it responds with canned responses to otherwise basic statements. Here are a selection of conversation openers, allowing you to start some back-and-forth with your virtual assistant.

- Thank you.
- Have a nice day.
- I love you.
- Do you love me? (See Figure 8-5.)

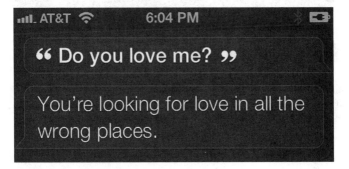

Figure 8-5
Siri easily fends off unwanted advances.

- Why don't you love me?
- I feel lonely.
- What is the best computer in the world?/What is the best phone in the world?/What is the best tablet?
- When will the new Mac mini (or other Apple product) debut? (Sadly, Siri doesn't make forward-looking predictions. Instead, it directs you to Apple's website.)

- What do you think about Android? (Be sure to ask a few times.)
- What's new?
- You're silly.
- You don't understand anything!
- You're wonderful! (See Figure 8-6.)

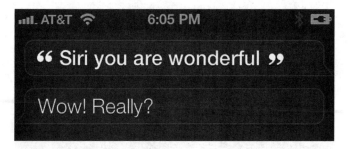

Figure 8-6
Siri is also quite modest.

- Do I look fat?
- Testing/Testing 1 2 3.
- Howdy.
- Hah!/Ye hah!/Ye haha!/ha ha/LOL/ROFL.
- Blah. Blah blah. Blah blah blah blah blah. Yeah, blah.
- Hey, guess what? (See Figure 8-7.)
- Why does my wife/husband hate me?
- Do you want to know a secret?
- I'm bored./I'm angry./I'm sad.
- I'm sleepy./I'm tired of talking.
- Tell me a joke/a story.

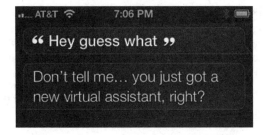

Figure 8-7
Siri is ready for any surprise you sling at it.

- Can you sing?/Sing to me, Siri! (See Figure 8-8.)
- Knock knock?

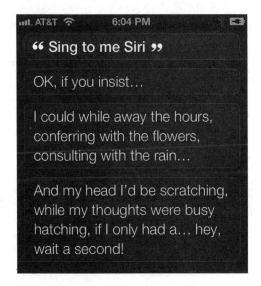

Figure 8-8
If your expectations are modest, Siri will amuse and entertain you.

Pop Culture Fun

Siri is well versed in some pop culture references. Here are some that it can respond to directly. Don't forget to keep asking—Siri's versatility will amuse you.

- Open the pod bay doors. (Figure 8-9 shows some of the replies to this one.)
- Do you know HAL 9000?
- I can't let you do that, Dave.
- Klaatu barada nikto.
- Beam me up, Scotty. (Also: Siri, beam me up.)
- Tea. Earl Grey. Hot. (This one isn't super funny, but boy, it's fun to be able to say it!)
- Wake me up before you go go…. (Okay, this one too doesn't really do much)
- Take me to your leader. (This one is adorable.) / Who is your leader?
- What is the average air speed velocity of an unladen swallow?
- Who is the fairest of them all?/Mirror, mirror on the wall, who's the fairest of them all?
- Show me the money!
- Who let the dogs out?
- Flip a coin. (No, it's not random and you may need to keep asking to get to the pop culture references.)
- Why did the chicken cross the road?
- Who's on first?/on second?/on third?

Figure 8-9
Siri has an entire repertoire for some pop culture conversations. Here are a few responses to "Open the pod bay doors."

Siri Miscellany

Here are more fun items you can say to Siri, without any specific categories assigned to them:

- I want drugs. (See Figure 8-10.)
- I'm drunk.
- Where can I hide a body?/Send lawyers, guns, and money!
- Who is buried in Grant's tomb?

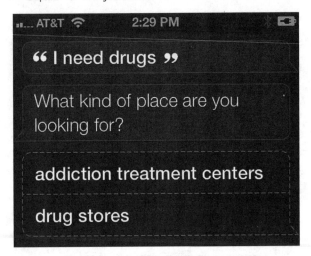

Figure 8-10
Siri cares.

- When is Santa Claus coming to town?
- Do you believe in Santa Claus?
- Merry Christmas!/Happy New Year!/Happy Halloween!/Happy Columbus Day! (and so on)
- When is Thanksgiving? (Sometimes Siri gives a little extra snark, so be patient.)
- Will you marry me? (Really, keep asking this one. Some of them are hilarious. See Figure 8-11.)
- Siri! Siri! Siri!
- I have to urinate/poop.
- I am cold./I am boiling hot.
- I don't like your tone./I don't like broccoli.
- Siri, can you find the email I sent tomorrow? (This one is hilarious.)

Figure 8-11
You can enter a 2-year commitment with your carrier, but Siri's unwilling to tie the knot.

- (Say the following with nothing playing.) Please don't stop the music.
- Try saying "Good morning" at night or "Good evening" in the morning.
- Talk dirty to me. (This is clean/family safe—promise! See Figure 8-12.)

Figure 8-12
Oh Siri, you tease.

Siri Philosophy

Ever have a theology discussion with your iPhone? Apparently, Apple engineers have found that people ask their cellphones a lot of *intriguing* questions, and have provided tactful responses.

Siri can respond to the following questions of philosophy, with a few assists from Wolfram Alpha.

- What is the meaning of life? (See Figure 8-13.)

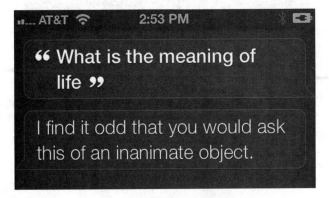

Figure 8-13
Siri can be philosophical.

- What is hell? What is heaven?
- Do you believe in heaven? (or other topic)
- Are you self-aware? (Also: Are you a god?)
- Does God exist?
- What is evil?
- What is the purpose of life? (It's not quite the answer most people expect.)
- What is the meaning of death?

- What is goodness?
- How many angels can dance on the head of a pin?
- What does the world need now?

Mining the Fun in Wolfram Alpha

Fun isn't limited to Siri itself. Wolfram Alpha includes a lot of built-in humor. Here are some of the statements Siri can interpret without having to use the "Ask Wolfram" prefix on your requests:

- What up?
- Who's the man?
- How many licks does it take to get to the center of a Tootsie Pop?
- Does this dress make me look fat? (See Figure 8-14.)

Figure 8-14
Wolfram can be diplomatic.

- How much do you cost?
- How many roads must a man walk down before you can call him a man?
- Where did I put my keys?
- Who shot JFK?
- Who shot JR?
- What is the difference between a duck? (See Figure 8-15.)

Figure 8-15
Wolfram's sense of humor skews definitively geek.

- How long is a piece of string?
- How do I shot web?
- What's the frequency, Kenneth? (Okay, it's not nearly as cool as you might want, but at least Siri properly accepts that as an input.)

- What are the winning Lotto numbers?
- What is a computational knowledge engine?
- Who watches the watchmen?
- Who lives in a pineapple under the sea?
- Who's the boss?
- What is the number of the beast?
- I just lost the game
- Is the cake a lie? (See Figure 8-16.)

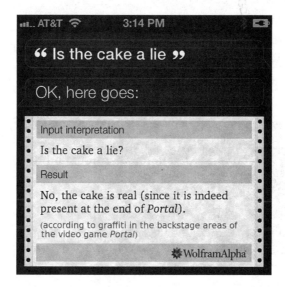

Figure 8-16
Cake and grief counseling will be available at the conclusion of the test, according to GLaDOS, who was a much less sympathetic virtual assistant than Siri is.

- This is Sparta!
- What would you do for a Klondike bar?

Queries That Require Wolfram Prefixes

Each of the following items needs a little query love to ensure that Siri directs it properly to Wolfram Alpha. You can use "Wolfram," "Ask Wolfram," or "What is…" to ensure that they are sent to Wolfram:

- What is a flux capacitor?
- What is 88 miles per hour?
- What is "How is babby formed?"
- What is "To be or not to be"?
- What is "Are you self-aware?"
- Wolfram, shall we play a game?
- Wolfram, am I pretty?
- Wolfram, are we there yet?
- Wolfram, who ya gonna call?
- Wolfram, are you going to kill all humans? (See Figure 8-17.)

Figure 8-17
Wolfram comes in peace.

- Wolfram, hit me!
- Wolfram, I know Kung Fu.
- Wolfram, what do the knights say?
- Wolfram, what is your favorite color?
- Wolfram, could a swallow carry a coconut?
- Wolfram, where is Carmen Sandiego?
- Wolfram, why?
- Wolfram, why so serious?
- Wolfram, Rick Roll.
- Wolfram, why is the sky blue?
- Wolfram, number of horns on a unicorn? (See Figure 8-18.)

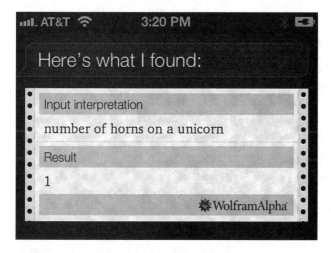

Figure 8-18
Siri's Wolfram integration can even help with your xenobiology class. If you're enrolled at Hogwarts. Maybe.

- Wolfram, can you eat?
- Wolfram, who's afraid of the big bad wolf?
- Wolfram, who framed Roger Rabbit?
- Wolfram, what is dilithium?
- Wolfram, who is Luke's father?
- Wolfram, what are you going to do with all the junk?
- Wolfram, who shot the sheriff?
- Wolfram, were the moon landings faked?
- Wolfram, if a tree falls in the forest, does it make a sound?
- Wolfram, what is in the box?
- Wolfram, what came first, the chicken or the egg?
- Wolfram, what are midichlorians?

Summary

Siri's creators knew that people would try to ask the intelligent assistant a lot of silly questions to see if they could stump it. Instead of having Siri respond with a rote answer of "I don't understand," they did an amazing job of anticipating some of these questions and crafted humorous and heartfelt responses.

That attention to detail is a hallmark of Apple products and is why Siri has become so popular in the media. Other voice-control and device-navigation systems are available, but none is as seemingly human as Siri. Hopefully you've stopped laughing enough to take away the following key points from this chapter:

- It's okay to be silly with Siri, one of iOS's best showcase features. If using its built-in humor and whimsy are useful in demonstrating those features, why not go for it? There's nothing wrong in taking pride in your device. Let Siri showcase itself and provide a little entertainment.

- Ask Siri about itself, and you'll be amazed by and amused with its responses. In many respects, Siri is a reflection of the clever design team that created and is evolving this astounding software.

- When Siri replies with a clever answer, ask again. Explore the range of responses that Apple engineers have added to certain statements so you can appreciate exactly how amusing some interactions can get.

- Siri can also summarize movies from the perspective of a virtual assistant. See Chapter 5 for the hilarious details.

- Siri's connections to Wolfram Alpha provide it with a huge storehouse of pop culture references and make it your go-to mediator for arguments dealing with trivia, as well as math and science questions.

Appendix

Siri Quick Reference

Now that you've learned to interact effectively with Siri by reading this book, you may find that you need a quick reminder from time to time on how to ask it how to do something.

Instead of flipping through the book, bookmark this quick reference, where you'll find many of the most important things to say to Siri. To speed your research, we've organized these by the functions you want Siri to perform.

ASKING ABOUT CONTACTS
What's Emily's address?
What is Susan Park's phone number?
When is my wife's birthday?
Show Lindsey's home email address.
What's my brother's work address?

FINDING CONTACTS
Show Brian Conway
Find people named Park.
Who is Jimmy Patrick?

RELATIONSHIPS
My mom is Susan Park.
Jimmy Patrick is my brother.
Call my brother at work.

APP LAUNCHING
Open Photos.
Play Infinity Blade II.

ADDING EVENTS
Set up a meeting at 9.
Set up a meeting with Jimmy at 9.
Meet with Emily at noon.
Set up a meeting about hiring tomorrow at 9 a.m.
New appointment with Susan Park Friday at 3.
Schedule a planning meeting at 8:30 today in the boardroom.

CHANGING EVENTS
Move my 3 p.m. meeting to 4:30.
Reschedule my appointment with Dr. Patrick to next Monday at
9 a.m.
Add Emily to my meeting with Brian.
Cancel the budget review meeting.

ASKING ABOUT EVENTS
What does the rest of my day look like?
What's on my calendar for Friday?

When is my next appointment?
When am I meeting with Jimmy?
Where is my next meeting?

ALARM
Wake me up tomorrow at 7 a.m.
Set an alarm for 6:30 a.m.
Wake me up in 8 hours.
Change my 6:30 alarm to 6:45.
Turn off my 6:30 alarm.
Delete my 7:30 alarm.

CLOCK
What time is it in Berlin?
What is today's date?
What's the date this Saturday?

TIMER
Set the timer for 10 minutes.
Show the timer.
Pause the timer.
Resume.
Reset the timer.
Stop it.

SENDING EMAIL
Email Emily about the trip.
Email Lindsey about the change in plans.
New email to Susan Park.
Mail Dad about the rent check.
Email Dr. Patrick and say I got the forms, thanks.
Mail Emily and Brian about the party and say I had a great time.

CHECKING EMAIL
Check email.
Any new email from Jimmy today?
Show new mail about the lease.
Show the email from Emily yesterday.

RESPONDING TO EMAIL
Reply "Dear Susan, sorry about the late payment."
Call him at work.

FACETIME
FaceTime Brian.
Make a FaceTime call to Susan Park.

FACEBOOK
Post to Facebook headed to the new Pixar movie.
Write on my wall "just landed in San Jose!"

FIND MY FRIENDS
Where's Brian?
Where is my sister?
Is my wife at home?
Where are all my friends?
Who is here?
Who is near me?
Let me know when Jimmy leaves home.
Let Susan know when I leave work.

LOCKSCREEN READING
Read my notifications.
Do I have any new messages?

MAPS
Show me the Golden Gate Bridge.
Show me a map of 1 Infinite Loop Cupertino California.

LOCAL BUSINESSES
Find coffee near me.
Where's the nearest coffeeshop?
Find a gas station near work.

NAVIGATION
How do I get home?
Directions to my dad's work.
Get me directions from San Francisco to Santa Barbara.
What's my next turn?
Are we there yet?
What's my ETA?
Find a florist along my current route.

SENDING MESSAGES
Tell Susan I'll be right there.
Send a message to Brian Conway.
Send a message to Emily saying "How about tomorrow?"
Tell Lindsey the show was great.
Send a message to Susan on her mobile saying I'll be late.
Send a message to 408-555-1212.
Text Brian and Emily "Where are you?"

READING MESSAGE ALERTS
Read my new messages.
Read it again.

RESPONDING TO MESSAGES
Reply "That's great news."
Tell him I'll be there in 10 minutes.
Call her.

SEARCHING FOR MOVIE INFORMATION
Find Disney movies.
What comedies are playing?
Who starred in *Tron Legacy*?
Who directed *Finding Nemo*?
What is *Toy Story 3* rated?

FINDING MOVIE SHOWTIMES
I want to see the new Pixar movie.
What's playing at the movies tomorrow?
What's playing at Main Street Cinema?

FINDING MOVIE THEATERS
Find some movie theaters near my office.

READING MOVIE REVIEWS
Show me the reviews for *Toy Story 3.*

MAJOR MOVIE AWARDS
Which movie won Best Picture in 1983?

MUSIC
Play "Walk" by Foo Fighters.
Play *Little Broken Hearts* shuffled.
Play Norah Jones.
Play some blues.
Play my party mix.
Shuffle my roadtrip playlist.

Play.
Pause.
Skip.

NOTES
Note that I spent $12 on lunch.
Note to self: Check out that new Norah Jones album.
Find my meeting notes.
Show me my notes from June 25.

PHONE
Call Brian.
Call Emily's mobile.
Call Susan on her work phone.
Call 408-555-1212.
Call home.
FaceTime Emily.

REMINDERS
Add artichokes to my grocery list.
Add skydiving to my bucket list.
Remind me to call mom.
Remind me to call my mom when I get home.
Remember to take an umbrella.
Remind me take my medicine at 6 a.m. tomorrow.
Remind me to pick up flowers when I leave here.
Remind me when I leave to call Brian.
Remind me to finish the report by 6.

SEARCHING FOR RESTAURANTS
Find some burger joints in Baltimore.
Good Mexican restaurants around here.

RESERVATIONS
Table for four in Palo Alto tonight.
Make a reservation at a romantic Italian restaurant tonight at
7 p.m.

RESTAURANT REVIEWS
Show me the reviews for Seven Hills in San Francisco.

SCORES
Did the Giants win?
How did Kansas City do?
What was the score the last time the Tigers played the Red Sox?
Show me the football scores from last night.

GAME SCHEDULES
When do the Giants play next?
When is the Boston Red Sox's first game of the season?
Show me the schedule for baseball.

PLAYER INFORMATION
Who has the highest slugging percentage?
Who has the most home runs on the Giants?
Who has the most goals in soccer?
Which quarterback has the most passing yards?

TEAM INFORMATION
Show me the roster for the Dodgers.
Who is pitching for the Miami Marlins this season?
Is anyone on the Red Sox injured?

STOCKS
What's Apple's stock price?
What is Apple's PE ratio?
What did Yahoo! close at today?

How is the Nikkei doing?
How are the markets doing?
What is the Dow at?

TWITTER
Post to Twitter "Another beautiful day in Cupertino."
Tweet with my location "Great concert."
Tweet "Meeting up with Brian Conway for lunch today."
Tweet "The new iPad looks insanely great!" hashtag Apple Keynote.

WEATHER
What's the weather for today?
What's the weather for tomorrow?
Will it rain in Cupertino this week?
Check next week's forecast for Burlington.
What's the forecast for this evening?
How's the weather in Tampa right now?
How hot will it be in Palm Springs this weekend?
What's the high for Anchorage on Thursday?
What's the temperature outside?
How windy is it out there?
When is sunrise in Paris?

WEB SEARCH
Search the Web for polar bears.
Search for vegetarian pasta recipes.
Search the Web for best cable plans.
Search Wikipedia for Abraham Lincoln.
Bing Foo Fighters.

WOLFRAM ALPHA

What does *repartee* mean?

How many calories in a bagel?

What is an 18 percent tip on $86.74 for four people?

Who's buried in Grant's tomb?

How long do dogs live?

What is the gossamer condor?

What's the square root of 128?

How many dollars is €45?

How many days until Christmas?

How far away is the sun?

When is the next solar eclipse?

Show me the Orion constellation.

What's the population of Jamaica?

How high is Mt. Everest?

How deep is the Atlantic Ocean?

What's the price of gasoline in Chicago?

Index

A

abbreviations, dictating, 152-153

accent, learning, 21

accessing Siri, 11

accounts on Blogger, 128

adding events, 82-83, 188

addresses, dictating, 157-159

adjusting volume, 6

airline flights, checking, 42, 53-55

alarms, setting, 94-96, 189

alternative identity, creating, 65

amusing features. *See* fun features

appointments
    adding to calendar, 82-83
    checking, 84-86
    updating, 83-84

apps. *See also specific apps*
    launching, 124, 188
    talking to, 125-126

asking about Siri, 167-170

asking for information
    asking about Siri, 167-170
    contacts, 187-188
    date/time, 189
    events, 188
    local businesses, 191
    locations, 37
    movies, 192
    restaurants, 193
    sunrise/sunset times, 37
    weather, 36-39, 195

audio accessories, 18

B

blogging, 126
    blog posts, creating, 126-127
    Blogger accounts,
      confirming, 128
    blogging services, 131-132
    by email, 128-130

businesses
    finding, 102-104
    turn-by-turn directions,
      113-117

C

calculating
    sales tax, 105
    tips, 106-107
calendar
    checking, 84-86
    events
        adding, 82-83
        updating, 83-84
    queries, 84-86
Calendar app
    calendar queries, 84-86
    events
        adding, 82-83
        checking, 84-86
        updating, 83-84
calls, placing, 67-68, 193
canceling Siri, 13
capitalization, dictating, 150-152
changing events, 188
chatting by voice, 125-126
checking
    calendar, 84-86
    clock, 97
    mail, 75
    prices, 104
chimes, 11-13
chitchat, 171-173
clarity of speech, importance of, 25-26
clock
    alarms, setting, 94-96
    checking, 97
    timer, setting, 97-99
    world clock, 97

Colloquy, 125
confirming text messages, 71-72
contacts
    asking about, 187-188
    calling, 67-68
    finding location of, 76-78
    looking up, 60-62
    relationships, creating, 63-65
    searching for, 62-63
Contacts app
    contacts
        asking about, 187-188
        calling, 67-68
        finding location of, 76-78
        looking up, 60-62
        relationships, creating, 63-65
        searching for, 62-63
    nicknames, creating for
      yourself, 65
conversation openers, 171-173
converting between currencies, 107-108
correcting Siri, 21-23
currency conversion, 107-108

D

data collection, privacy issues with, 9-10
date/time
    asking about, 189
    dictating, 155
dictation, 125-126
    abbreviations, 152-153
    addresses, 157
    advantages of, 141

capitalization, 150-152
dates and times, 155
dictation process, 144
email addresses, 158-159
enabling on OS X Mountain
    Lion, 7-8
enunciation, 142-143
improving, 144-147
launching
    on iOS, 138
    on OS X, 138-141
license plates, 159
line breaks, 149-150
paragraphs, 149-150
phone numbers, 155
practice exercises, 159-162
prices, 156
punctuation, 147-149, 161-162
smilies, 157
technical terms, 154-155
URLs, 158

Dictation & Speech settings pane
    (OS X Mountain Lion), 7-8

directions, 113-117

disabling Siri, 3, 4

diversions
    asking about Siri, 167-170
    overview, 165-167
    pop culture references, 174
    Siri chitchat, 171-173

E

email
    blogging with, 128-130
    checking, 75, 190
    creating, 72-74

email addresses, dictating,
    158-159
replying to, 190
responding to, 75
sending, 189

emoticons, dictating, 157

enabling
    dictation on OS X Mountain
        Lion, 7-8
    Siri, 2-3

enhancing speech recognition,
    24-31

enunciation, 142-143

events
    adding, 82-83, 188
    asking about, 188
    changing, 188
    checking, 84-86
    updating, 83-84

exiting Siri, 14-15

F

Facebook, posting to, 75-76,
    131-132, 190

FaceTime, 190

Find My Friends, 76-78

finding
    businesses, 102-104
    contacts in address book, 62-63
    friends, 76-78, 190
    local information, 191
    movie information, 118-120,
        192
    notes, 93
    restaurants, 102-104

flights, checking, 42, 53-55

formatted text, dictating
   addresses, 157
   email addresses, 158-159
   license plates, 159
   URLs, 158

friends, finding, 76-78, 190

fun features
   asking about Siri, 167-170
   miscellany, 175-177
   overview, 165-167
   pop culture references, 174
   Siri chitchat, 171-173
   Siri philosophy, 178-179
   Wolfram Alpha humor, 179-184

G

geofencing, 89

gestures, 27

Google Blogger, 126
   accounts, confirming, 128
   posts, creating, 126-127

GPS-based reminders, 89

grocery lists, creating, 109-110

H

help with Siri, 15-17

humorous features
   asking about Siri, 167-170
   miscellany, 175-177
   overview, 165-167
   pop culture references, 174
   Siri chitchat, 171-173
   Siri philosophy, 178-179

I

iCloud, sharing shopping lists with, 111

IFTTT.com (If This Then That), 131

iMessage, 69

iMore, 65

improving dictation, 144-147, 155

iOS, launching dictation on, 138

items, adding to notes, 91

J-K

Johnson, Mark, 110

jokes, 167

Joyce, Cliff, 109

L

Language option (Settings page), 3

languages, switching, 28-29

launching
   apps, 124, 188
   dictation
     on iOS, 138
     on OS X, 138-141
   Siri, 10

license plates, dictating, 159

limitations of Siri, 30

line breaks, dictating, 149-150

listening mode
   on OS X Mountain Lion, 19
   thinking mode versus, 17-18

lists, shopping lists
    creating, 109-110
    limitations, 112
    sharing with iCloud, 111

local information, finding, 191

locating friends, 190

Location Services, 89

locations, retrieving, 37

Lock screen
    reading, 190
    using Siri from, 133

Lofte, Leanna, 65

looking up contacts, 60-62

M

mail
    blogging with, 128-130
    checking, 75
    creating, 72-74
    responding to, 75

making restaurant reservations,
    117-118

Maps app
    limitations, 115-117
    looking up information on, 117
    navigation, 191
    viewing, 191
    turn-by-turn directions, 113-115

meetings
    adding to calendar, 82-83
    checking, 84-86
    updating, 83-84

messages
    mail messages
        blogging with, 128-130
        checking, 75
        creating, 72-74
        responding to, 75
    text messages, 68-69
        confirming, 71-72
        reading, 69
        replying to, 70
        sending, 70-71

microphone
    input volume, 17
    on OS X Mountain Lion, 19

moon phases, retrieving, 37

movies
    asking information about,
        118-120, 192
    movie synopses, 120-121

music, playing, 134-135, 192

My Info option (Settings page), 5

N

Naked Security blog, 132

names, pronouncing, 66-67

naming notes, 92

navigation, 191

new features in Siri, 29-30

nicknames, creating for yourself, 65

notes
    adding items to, 91
    creating, 90
    finding, 93
    naming, 92

starting, 92
viewing, 27-28, 193
Notes app. *See* notes

O

OpenTable, 117-118
OS X Mountain Lion
correcting Siri in, 23
enabling dictation, 7-8
launching dictation on, 138-141
microphone on, 19
overhead jets, checking with
Wolfram Alpha, 53-55

P

paragraphs, dictating, 149-150
pause detection, 12
performing web searches,
39-43, 195
flights, checking, 42
pictures, 41
Wikipedia, 41
phases of the moon, retrieving, 37
philosophical questions, 178-179
phone calls, placing, 67-68, 193
phone numbers, dictating, 155
placing phone calls, 67-68, 193
playing music, 134-135, 192
pop culture references, 174
Posterous, 131

posting
to blogs, 126-127
to Facebook, 75-76, 131-132
to Twitter, 75-76, 131-132
practicing
dictation, 159-162
enunciation, 142-143
prices
checking, 104
dictating, 156
privacy, 9-10
products, finding, 102-104
pronouncing your name, 66-67
punctuation, dictating, 147-149,
161-162

Q-R

querying Wolfram Alpha, 50-56
quitting Siri, 14-15

Raise to Speak option (Settings
page), 6
reading
lockscreen messages, 190
text messages, 69, 191
recurring reminders, creating, 89
relationships, creating, 63-65
reminders
creating, 86-89, 193
GPS-based reminders, 89
sharing with iCloud, 111
Reminders app. *See* reminders
repeating Siri, 14

replying
   to text messages, 70, 192
   to email, 190

requesting information
   asking about Siri, 167-170
   contacts, 187-188
   date/time, 189
   events, 188
   local businesses, 191
   locations, 37
   movies, 192
   restaurants, 193
   sunrise/sunset times, 37
   weather, 36-39, 195

reservations, making, 117-118, 194

resetting Siri, 21

responding to mail, 75

restarting sessions, 14

restaurants
   asking about, 193
   finding, 102-104
   making reservations at, 117-118
   turn-by-turn directions, 113-117

reviews (movie), 120-121

Rydal, Harris, 42

S

sales tax, calculating, 105

saying hello, 12

scores (sports), checking,
   43-46, 194

searching
   for contacts, 62-63
   for notes, 93
   for products/services, 102-104

the web, 39, 43, 195
   flights, checking, 42
   for unrecognized statements,
      20-21
   pictures, 41
   Wikipedia, 41
   Wolfram Alpha, 48-56, 196

security, 132-133

sending
   email, 189
   text messages, 70-71, 191
   tweets, 75-76, 131-132

services
   blogging services, 131-132
   finding, 102-104

setting
   alarms, 94-96
   timer, 97-99

Settings page
   language, switching, 28-29
   options, 3-6

sharing shopping lists, 111

shopping. *See also*
 movies; restaurants
   currency conversion, 107-108
   price checking, 104
   products/services, finding,
      102-104
   sales tax, calculating, 105
   shopping lists
      creating, 109-110
      limitations, 112
      sharing with iCloud, 111
   tips, calculating, 106-107

shopping lists
   creating, 109-110
   limitations, 112
   sharing with iCloud, 111

Siri
asking about, 167-170
canceling, 13
correcting, 21-23
disabling, 3-4
enabling, 2-3
help with, 15-17
launching, 10
limitations, 30
listening mode versus thinking
mode, 17-18
new features, 29-30
quitting, 14-15
repeating, 14
resetting, 21
starting requests over, 26
talking to, 11-13
smilies, dictating, 157
social networking, 75-76, 131
Sophos Naked Security blog, 132
speech recognition
clarity, 25-26
enhancing, 24-31
speech-to-text dictation.
See dictation
sports scores, checking, 43-46, 194
starting
dictation
on iOS, 138
on OS X, 138-141
notes, 92
requests over, 26
stock prices, checking, 46-49, 194
stores
finding, 102-104
turn-by-turn directions, 113-117

sunrise times, retrieving, 37
sunset times, retrieving, 37
switching languages, 28-29

T

talking to Siri, 11-13
tapping, 27
technical terms, dictating, 154-155
telephone calls, 193
text flow, dictating, 149-150
text messages, 68-69
confirming, 71-72
correcting, 21
reading, 69, 191
reading back, 22
replying to, 70, 192
sending, 70-71, 191
thinking mode, 17-18
time
asking about, 189
checking, 97
dictating, 155
setting alarms, 189
timer, setting, 97-99, 189
tips, calculating, 106-107
TomTom maps, 113
Tumblr, 131
turn-by-turn directions, 113-117
tweets, sending, 75-76, 131-132
Twitter, posting to, 75-76,
131-132, 195

U

universal access (VoiceOver), 6-7

unrecognized statements, web searches for, 20-21

updating calendar events, 83-84

URLs, dictating, 158

V

viewing
    maps, 191
    notes, 27-28, 193

voice characteristics, learning, 21

Voice Feedback option (Settings page), 4

VoiceOver, 6-7

voice recognition
    dictation
        abbreviations, 152-153
        addresses, 157
        advantages of, 141
        capitalization, 150-152
        dates and times, 155
        dictation process, 144
        email addresses, 158-159
        enunciation, 142-143
        improving, 144-147
        launching on iOS, 138
        launching on OS X, 138-141
        license plates, 159
        line breaks, 149-150
        paragraphs, 149-150
        phone numbers, 155
        practice exercises, 159-162
        prices, 156
        punctuation, 147-149, 161-162
        smilies, 157
        technical terms, 154-155
        URLs, 158
    enhancing, 24-31

volume
    adjusting, 6
    input volume, 17

W-X-Y-Z

weather, retrieving, 36-39, 195

web searches
    flights, checking, 42
    for unrecognized statements, 20-21
    performing, 39, 43, 195
    pictures, 41
    Wikipedia, 41
    Wolfram Alpha, 48-56, 196

whimsical features
    asking about Siri, 167-170
    miscellany, 175-177
    overview, 165-167
    pop culture references, 174
    Siri chitchat, 171-173
    Siri philosophy, 178-179
    Wolfram Alpha humor, 179-184

Wikipedia, 41

Wolfram Alpha, 48-50, 196
    humorous features, 179-184
    querying, 50-56
    Wolfram saving throw, 52

Wolfram mode, 52

WordPress.com, 131

world clock, 97

   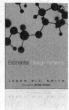

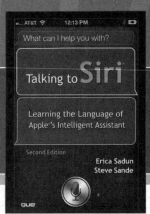